Withdrawn

D1356398

Social Change in a Metropolitan Community

SOCIAL CHANGE
IN A
METROPOLITAN COMMUNITY

Otis Dudley Duncan
Howard Schuman
Beverly Duncan

Russell Sage Foundation   *New York*

PUBLICATIONS OF RUSSELL SAGE FOUNDATION

Russell Sage Foundation was established in 1907 by Mrs. Russell Sage for the improvement of social and living conditions in the United States. In carrying out its purpose the Foundation conducts research under the direction of members of the staff or in close collaboration with other institutions, and supports programs designed to develop and demonstrate productive working relations between social scientists and other professional groups. As an integral part of its operation, the Foundation from time to time publishes books or pamphlets resulting from these activities. Publication under the imprint of the Foundation does not necessarily imply agreement by the Foundation, its Trustees, or its staff with the interpretations or conclusions of the authors.

HN
80
· D6 D86

Russell Sage Foundation
230 Park Avenue, New York, N.Y. 10017

© 1973 by Russell Sage Foundation. All Rights Reserved.
Library of Congress Catalog Card Number: 73–76764
Standard Book Number: 87154–216–1 (Paperbound edition)
                      87154–217–X (Hardcover edition)
Printed in the United States of America by Connecticut Printers, Inc., Hartford, Connecticut

Contents

1015632

Foreword

It was during 1967–1969 that Otis Dudley Duncan and I had several opportunities to discuss the emergence and development of a sub-field of social science investigation—that which is now commonly referred to as "social indicators." In one product of these discussions[1] Duncan presented an elegant case for employing "replications of baseline studies" as a strategy for developing measurements of social change. In a 1971 omnibus survey, Duncan, the other authors of this volume, and their colleagues carefully replicated a set of social facts initially observed in the Detroit Area Studies dating from 1953 through 1959. An impressive record of social change covering a variety of topics from the 1950s to 1971 resulted and is presented here.

Social Change in a Metropolitan Community is the eighth in a series of Russell Sage Foundation publications (Eleanor Bernert Sheldon and Wilbert E. Moore, *Indicators of Social Change: Concepts and Measurements,* 1968; Abbott L. Ferriss, *Indicators of Trends in American Education,* 1969; Abbott L. Ferriss, *Indicators of Change in the American Family,* 1970; Abbott L. Ferris, *Indicators of Trends in the Status of American Women,* 1971; Otis Dudley Duncan, *Toward Social Reporting: Next Steps,* 1969; Angus Campbell and Philip E. Converse, *The Human Meaning of Social Change,* 1972; Peter J. Henriot, *Political Aspects of Social Indicators: Implications for Research,* 1972) pertaining to the measurement of social change. Both its simplicity of presentation and sophisticated understanding of the complexities of its subject matter mark this volume

[1] Otis Dudley Duncan, *Toward Social Reporting: Next Steps.* Social Science Frontiers Series, New York: Russell Sage Foundation, 1969.

as an important contribution not only to the Foundation's program but also to the ever-widening endeavor of research on social change.

ELEANOR BERNERT SHELDON

New York City
July 1973

The Study

The subject of social change is much discussed these days, both by those who put forward "demands for meaningful change in the system" and those who regret the seeming "erosion of values embodied in the traditions of our national life." There can be no doubt that things really are changing, whatever our individual desires for change may be. Yet, when so much is in flux, it is not easy to be sure exactly what is going on. Casual observers may secure biased impressions and commentators may stress selectively the sensational aspects of change. While interpretations of change and reactions to change will necessarily differ from one person to another, there is need for reliable observations of change to provide a sound and widely accepted factual basis for public discussion.

This report submits a substantial body of social facts obtained by a well-developed and time-tested method—the sample survey of a human population. Although there is general appreciation of the capabilities of surveys, this method has not been exploited as much as it might be for the purpose of recording and analyzing social change. In undertaking this study, it was our intention to demonstrate the potential usefulness of the survey method for this purpose and at the same time to generate measurements of some important changes occurring in a metropolitan community during the past two decades.

A project of this kind was feasible because of the work of previous investigators. Since 1952, the Detroit Area Study, a facility for training graduate students in social research at the University of Michigan, has carried out an annual study in metropolitan Detroit. By repeating portions of a survey done in 1956, for example, we could secure comparative measurements spanning a 15-year period. Nearly all of our 1971 survey was based on this procedure, replication of items drawn from the original (base-line) surveys. We took special interest in the surveys done each year from 1953 through 1959 for two reasons: first, select-

1

ing them for base-line purposes maximized the time span over which change might be measured; and, second, for various technical reasons the replication was easier to accomplish than would have been the case for some of the surveys done during the 1960s. For one particular topic, racial attitudes, we used base-line data from later surveys.

In regard to the topics to be studied—or, aspects of change to be measured—our approach was opportunistic and eclectic. We simply considered each question asked in a base-line survey as a potential item in the new study and required it to pass some obvious tests: it should not be too dated by its wording or subject matter (as, for example, a question on preference for Eisenhower or Stevenson); it should be relevant to some problem of current public concern or to some continuing issue of sociological theory; it should be the kind of question that would be manageable in a long interview covering diverse subjects. All items were pretested and those causing serious difficulty in understanding were dropped. Our aim was to explore as many different aspects of change as possible, even if that required some sacrifice of depth on particular topics. Thus, we were not able to use all the questions from the earlier surveys that seemed to merit replication.

While our measurements pertain to a variety of topics, there are many aspects of social change we could not attempt to cover. The professional social scientist reading this report will find estimates of change in many characteristics and responses for which such estimates have never before been available. At the same time, the general reader may wonder why our coverage of significant trends is not broader. Our hope is that future studies, both those using a strategy similar to ours and those taking different approaches, will indeed broaden the base of information about trends. Needless to say, the things we would *like* to know about social change will always outnumber those we think we *do* know.

This report is comprehensive in that it provides a statistical summary for almost all the items included in the 1971 survey. The summary is not, however, highly analytical. Most of the interpretations suggested are somewhat superficial, and some may be changed after we complete a detailed statistical analysis. In this report, however, we have tried to be sure that the changes described are statistically reliable even if their causation and implications may be obscure. Although there is no display of the apparatus of statistical inference, chi-square tests have been carried out in all cases to rule out the possibility that an ostensible change might easily have resulted from mere accidents of random sampling. Unless there is indication to the contrary, differences between years discussed in the text are statistically significant at the nominal .05 level of probability. However, we do not wish to stress unduly the problem of sampling error, since there are various other obstacles to correct inference—some of which are pointed out along the way—that are equally important.

In the 1971 survey the interviewers associated with the project—students in the Detroit Area Study and professional interviewers on the staff of the Survey Research Center, University of Michigan—visited 2,344 randomly selected sample addresses and secured interviews at 1,881 of them, for a response rate of 80 percent. The several base-line studies had response rates varying between 82 percent and 87 percent, but the sample sizes were considerably smaller. Moreover, some of the earlier studies were limited to designated subpopulations. In this report we compare results on our full sample of 1,881 with results from an earlier survey when that survey covered a complete cross-section of the adult population as did the 1971 survey. When the base-line survey pertained to a subpopulation, we constructed a comparable subsample from the 1971 study by eliminating those respondents who would not have been eligible under the rules of the earlier survey. In addition to the interviews with 1,881 respondents in 1971, we used data from the following sources:

568 mothers of children under 19 years, 1953
764 adults (cross-section), 1954
731 wives living with their husbands, 1955

797 adults (cross-section), 1956
596 adults (cross-section) living in Wayne County, 1957
656 adults (cross-section), 1958
767 adults (cross-section), 1959
600 black adults (household heads and wives) living in the city of Detroit, 1968
631 white adults (household heads and wives), 1969.

Except in 1957 and 1968, these surveys, like the 1971 survey, covered all of Wayne County (which contains the city of Detroit) and the contiguous, heavily urbanized sections of Macomb and Oakland counties.

Our tables usually are based upon somewhat smaller numbers than those just given, for several reasons. In some of the surveys (1953, 1959, 1971) certain questions were asked only of a randomly selected half of the respondents. In all of the studies each question was left unanswered by a few respondents; and a few others gave answers that could not be classified. The subject matter of certain questions limits their applicability to particular segments of the population. These limits will be explicit in the tables given in this study, but we have not otherwise called attention to the variations in numbers of cases arising from the other sources. As previously stated, we carried out statistical tests of the significance of change which are intended to make allowance for the increased sampling variation that goes with small samples.

Almost all the figures shown in this report, other than those attributed to published sources, derive from our own tabulations from the 1971 and the base-line studies. Minor discrepancies from the results reported in the studies by the original investigators were encountered, as was to be expected on the basis of previous experience in working with complex data files. We did not find serious discrepancies of the kind requiring substantial modifications in our statements of findings. All interpretations of the base-line data are, however, our own and are not the responsibility of the original research workers.

The reader who would like to have additional technical details about the study, or who is interested in the few particular topics that we have analyzed more fully elsewhere, is referred to the following:

Elizabeth M. Fischer, *Sampling Report for the 1971 Detroit Area Study* (Detroit Area Study, University of Michigan, 1972).

Beverly Duncan and Mark Evers, "Measuring Change in Attitudes toward Women's Work," Conference on Social Indicator Models, Russell Sage Foundation, July 1972.

Otis Dudley Duncan, "Measuring Social Change via Replication of Surveys," Conference on Social Indicator Models, Russell Sage Foundation, July 1972.

Howard Schuman, "Two Sources of Antiwar Sentiment in America," *American Journal of Sociology*, 78 (November 1972): 513–536.

Howard Schuman, *Trends and Complexities in Black Racial Attitudes*, Institute for Social Research, University of Michigan (forthcoming).

Marriage

Most of our material on changes in marriage takes the wife's point of view since in the principal base-line study dealing with marriage only wives were interviewed. The questions were framed to elicit their reports on the marriage relationship and their evaluations of marriage in general or their own marriage in particular. It would be interesting to know if wives and husbands seek the same things in marriage and if the two sexes are finding equal gratification (or frustration!) in marriage, but unfortunately our data do not deal with these questions.

VALUES IN MARRIAGE

It may be that most adults marry because this is the conventional and expected thing to do. Yet, even this most traditional of human institutions is, in modern times, asked to serve individual human purposes. Our respondents had little difficulty telling us what values women might hope to realize in marrying. Table 1 reveals a pronounced change, in just sixteen years, in the relative importance of some of these values. Both in 1955 and in 1971 a plurality of wives put companionship with the husband as the top value, but the plurality of 48 percent in 1955 expanded to a strong majority of 60 percent in 1971. The second leading value in 1955 was the chance to have children, and a quarter (26 percent) of the women regarded it as the most valuable part of marriage; but this fraction was reduced to 13 percent in 1971, and the chance to have children was tied with the husband's understanding for second place. The entire change in relative popularity of the five choices allowed by the question can be described by the gain for companionship, compensated by the loss for chance to have children. The remaining three, husband's understanding, husband's affection, and the standard of living, retained their relative positions and respective shares of the first choices.

Table 1. Values in Marriage

Thinking of marriage in general, which one of these five things would you say is the most valuable part of marriage?	Percent Distribution of Wives	
	1955	1971
The chance to have children	26	13
The standard of living—the kind of house, clothes, car, and so forth	3	3
The husband's understanding of the wife's problems and feelings	13	13
The husband's expression of love and affection for the wife	10	11
Companionship in doings things together with the husband	48	60
	100	100

The question actually requested the wives to designate their second and third choices as well. A study of the distributions of these choices does not particularly alter the summary already given. It turns out that nearly all the wives included either companionship or the chance to have children, or both, among their first three choices. Considering the three choices, we find that 64 percent put companionship ahead of the chance to have children in 1955, but 79 percent did so in 1971.

It is significant that the same kind of change occurred for wives with various social characteristics: for younger and older, for black and white, for well educated and less well educated wives, there was a drop in the emphasis on the chance to have children and a rise in the value of companionship. There are, of course, some differences in the extent of change. For example, in 1955, Catholic wives were somewhat more likely than Protestant to put first the chance to have children, but by 1971, the Catholic proportion having dropped faster, there was little difference. In this report, we will not comment on such detailed variations in the trends discerned, unless they appear to be critical in making an interpretation.

Consistent with the lower evaluation of the chance to

have children, wives' opinions as to the ideal number of children showed a substantial change. In 1955, three- and four-child families were the most frequently mentioned (see Table 2), while in 1971 the two-child family, mentioned by just half the women, was by far the most popular choice. The distribution of sizes selected implied an average (mean) of 3.3 children per family in 1955, as compared to 2.6 in 1971. Incidentally, the ideal number of children as given by the wives is much the same as that given by all adults; the averages are the same to one decimal point (2.6) in 1971. We infer that the shift in opinion toward a more favorable view of the small family has been pervasive and not confined to women.

The results mentioned here refer to the ideal size of the "average American family." When the question is phrased somewhat differently, to refer to "a young couple if their standard of living is about like yours," respondents recommend somewhat smaller sizes. Again, however, we find a pronounced shift (second question, Table 2). In

Table 2. Ideal Number of Children

		Percent Distribution					
		Less than 2	2	*3*[a]	*4*	*More than* 4	*Total*
As things are now, what do you think is the ideal number of children for the average American family?	Wives						
	1955	1	22	34	36	7	100
	1971	4	51	26	16	3	100
	All adults						
	1971	3	52	27	14	4	100
In your opinion what would be the ideal number of children for a young couple to have if their standard of living is about like yours?	All adults						
	1954	7	33	31	23	6	100
	1971	14	52	21	10	3	100

[a] Includes "2 or 3" and "3 or 4."

1954, the average of the sizes suggested by respondents was 2.9; in 1971, 2.3. In both years, many respondents evidently felt that their own standard of living was not high enough to provide support for as many children as might otherwise be desirable. But the estimate of change in ideal family size is hardly affected by inserting the reference to the standard of living.

In an unpublished paper, Barry Edmonston has shown that the changes in ideal number of children recorded by the Detroit Area Study (in addition to the years considered here, there are data for 1952 and for special subpopulations in 1962 and 1966) are closely parallel to the changes shown by national polls and surveys. The comparisons with the national data provide a closer estimate of the actual timing of the change than we can secure from the Detroit data alone. There was a gradual decrease in the average ideal number of children between the late 1950s and mid-1960s, followed by a more precipitous drop after 1965 or 1966. The documented similarity between Detroit and national data on this particular topic suggests to us, though it does not prove, that our findings on changes in other domains may be at least broadly representative of what has been happening in the nation as a whole, or at least in the larger metropolitan areas of the North.

Four of the values in marriage in Table 1 are considered again in Table 3, not in terms of marriage in general, but with reference to the wife's own marriage. She was asked to rate her degree of satisfaction with each designated aspect of the marriage on a five-point scale. It is encouraging to report that the most frequent response is "quite satisfied," that more wives are "enthusiastic" than are "pretty disappointed" with their marriages, and that these patterns hold in both years. The skeptical reader may wonder if dissatisfied wives are as willing to report their feelings as satisfied ones and whether to accept at face value the finding that a majority of wives are quite satisfied or enthusiastic. For purposes of estimating change, however, we need not assume that the categories have an absolute meaning, but only that they communicate the re-

Table 3. Wives' Satisfaction with Marriage (Percent Distribution)

... how you feel about each of the following:		*Degree of Satisfaction*[a]					
		1 (*Low*)	*2*	*3*	*4*	*5* (*High*)	*Total*
Your standard of living ... the kind of house, clothes, and so forth?	1955	3	19	19	54	5	100
	1971[b]	1	20	16	56	7	100
The understanding you get of your problems and feelings?	1955	4	11	30	43	12	100
	1971[b]	6	11	27	44	12	100
The love and affection you receive?	1955	2	5	19	43	31	100
	1971	5	8	14	42	31	100
The companionship in doing things together?	1955	4	11	17	38	30	100
	1971	7	12	14	40	27	100

[a] Response alternatives:
1. Pretty disappointed—I'm really missing out on that.
2. It would be nice to have more.
3. It's all right, I guess—I can't complain.
4. Quite satisfied—I'm lucky the way it is.
5. Enthusiastic—It couldn't be better.
[b] Difference between years not significant.

spondents' feelings in the same way in 1971 as in 1955. If this were not so, it would be difficult to understand how the distributions could be so similar, especially for the two items for which the 1971 distribution is not significantly different from the 1955 distribution—the standard of living, and the husband's understanding.

For the other two items, the husband's affection and companionship with the husband, the 1955 and 1971 distributions again are similar. Nevertheless, the shift to the two lowest categories, although it involves a tiny minority of wives, shows up as statistically reliable. Inasmuch as companionship has assumed so clearly the topmost position in the hierarchy of values, it is disquieting that a few more wives—19 percent in 1971, as against 15 percent in 1955—report that they are pretty disappointed or that it would be nice to have more. It may be, however, that disappointment is most likely where expectations are highest.

It is possible, too, that we have picked up the beginning of a trend that will gain momentum as more and more wives come to feel that their own marriages do not allow them to realize the values they put highest. But this is only speculation about the future. What we can say about the trend to date is that dissatisfaction with marriage has not developed at nearly the pace that is evident in regard to certain other institutions we will discuss later.

DIVISION OF LABOR AND DECISION-MAKING

Our questions on values in marriage did not further define "companionship in doing things together with the husband," so that we do not know whether the wives had in mind activities outside the home and the daily routine of household life, or whether they included in "companionship" the sharing of household duties with the spouse. In either event, there is interest for its own sake in the question of how wives and husbands organize the work that must be done.

The division of labor between spouses in the household comprises a great many tasks and decisions, some large and some small. The spouse who makes more of the "important" decisions may be seen as the one with the greater "power." But sometimes, we suspect, the person who usually gets to make the decision is the one who has the occasion to do so. No doubt some couples self-consciously adopt an equalitarian approach to the division of labor. Even when this happens, we may not be able to infer exactly who will do what. One equalitarian approach would be to trade off, so that if wife does task A, husband does task B. Another approach is for both to do each of tasks A and B about half the time, or for the two spouses to do the tasks together—provided the tasks are amenable to joint performance. Other couples, of course, may not seek to equalize the wife's and husband's burdens, but rather follow some conventional idea of which kinds of duties and decisions are appropriate to which sex. For still other couples, the division of labor is worked out over time in an expedient fashion, reflecting in part the skills and inter-ests of each partner, and in part the other demands on her or his time and effort.

In the opinion of Blood and Wolfe, authors of the study from which we draw our 1955 data, the transition from a patriarchal to a relatively equalitarian pattern of marriage occurred well before the middle of this century.[1] If that transition lies so far in the past, then the disappear-ance of patriarchy will not forecast much about current changes. As we shall see, those changes include several distinct trends, most of them fairly minor variations on the general pattern of the division of labor.

Our data pertain to a dozen items commonly included on the continuing agenda of husband-wife households. These items are only a sampling of the tasks and decisions that spouses regularly face, and may not be representative of others on which we lack information. The patterns of change are heterogeneous: for all but two of the items there is a clear shift in the division of labor, but the kinds of shifts are varied. Hence, we must consider the items one at a time.

(1) In Table 4 we see a substantial increase in the proportion of homes where the grocery shopping is always the wife's job, but there has been no significant change in the relative sizes of the other four categories.

(2) Getting breakfast now is much more frequently the husband's job than in 1955, and is much less frequently done exclusively by the wife (the intermediate categories show no relative change).

(3) Doing the evening dishes was and remains the task most clearly monopolized by the wife. The data even suggest that she is in complete charge of this function more often now than earlier, but the change is not large enough to register statistical significance.

(4) Straightening up the living room has a fairly similar distribution to doing dishes and similarly shows

---

[1] Robert O. Blood, Jr. and Donald M. Wolfe, *Husbands and Wives* (New York: Free Press, 1960).

Table 4. Performance of Household Tasks by Spouses (Percent Distribution)

We would like to know how you and your husband divide up some of the family jobs:		Percent of Married Women Saying					
		Husband always	Husband more	Exactly the same	Wife more	Wife always	Total
Who does the grocery shopping?	1955	7	7	29	20	37	100
	1971	7	5	22	19	47	100
Who gets your husband's breakfast on work days?	1955	16	5	4	7	68	100
	1971	29	4	4	7	56	100
Who does the evening dishes?	1955	1	2	14	12	71	100
	1971[a]	1	1	11	12	75	100
Who straightens up the living room when company is coming?	1955	1	1	17	15	66	100
	1971	2	<1	18	15	65	100
Who repairs things around the house?	1955	75	12	7	3	3	100
	1971	64	16	8	5	7	100
Who keeps track of the money and bills?	1955	19	7	34	11	29	100
	1971	23	7	24	10	36	100

[a] Difference between years is not statistically significant.

but a slight change. There is, however, a significant increase in the proportion of husbands who always handle this job, although that proportion remains tiny.

(5) Repairing things around the house remains predominantly the husband's task, but it is less exclusively his now than it was in 1955. The other four categories describing the allocation of this task have increased proportionally at the expense of "husband always."

(6) Keeping track of the money and bills was shared equally by the two spouses in one-third of the households in 1955, but only in one-quarter of them in 1971. The shift in responsibility has gone in both directions, so that both "husband always" and "wife always" are reported more frequently in 1971.

The division of influence with regard to certain economic and household decisions is shown in Table 5.

(1) In 1971 as in 1955, deciding what car to buy was primarily the husband's prerogative, and there has been no change in the proportions of couples dividing the responsibility for this decision in various ways.

(2) Whether to buy life insurance has become more exclusively the husband's decision; the category, "husband always," gained at the expense of each of the other categories over the sixteen-year period covered by these data.

(3) The selection of a house or apartment is the decision most often shared exactly the same by husband and wife. But the change is toward the husband's assuming this responsibility more often and the wife less often.

(4) What job he should take is something the husband usually decides by himself. Yet, there is some change in how this function is allocated, for the other four categories gained proportionally, between 1955 and 1971, at the expense of "husband always."

(5) The counterpart to the foregoing is the indication that fewer women now decide by themselves whether or not to work. The decision was more often shared equally with the husband in 1971 than in 1955.

(6) Figuring out how much money to spend on food is a task that tends to go with doing the grocery shopping

Table 5. Decision-Making by Spouses (Percent Distribution)

Who usually makes the final decision about:		Percent of Married Women Saying					
		Husband always	Husband more	Exactly the same	Wife more	Wife always	Total
What car to get?	1955	57	13	25	2	3	100
	1971[a]	58	10	26	1	5	100
Whether or not to buy some life insurance?	1955	32	11	42	5	10	100
	1971	43	10	36	3	8	100
What house or apartment to take?	1955	13	6	58	10	13	100
	1971	17	6	63	5	9	100
What job your husband should take?	1955	91	5	3	0	1	100
	1971	87	8	4	<1	1	100
Whether or not you should go to work or quit work?	1955	27	5	19	9	40	100
	1971	26	5	24	10	35	100
How much money your family can afford to spend per week on food?	1955	10	3	33	12	42	100
	1971	14	3	34	7	42	100

[a] Difference between years is not statistically significant.

and thus one that is usually undertaken by the wife. Yet, between 1955 and 1971 the rather small proportion of couples assigning this decision to the "husband always" underwent a significant increase.

Clearly, these diverse results do not point to some monolithic trend either toward greater sharing of tasks and decisions or toward greater specialization of sex roles in the household division of labor. On the contrary, one has the impression that rather small adjustments are being made without altering the general principles upon which couples work out their respective roles. Figure 1 provides a more succinct representation of the changes described and tends to confirm this impression. The dozen items considered here are located on the chart in such a way that a shift to the lower left of the diagram means that "husband always" has gained in its proportion; a shift to the lower right simi-

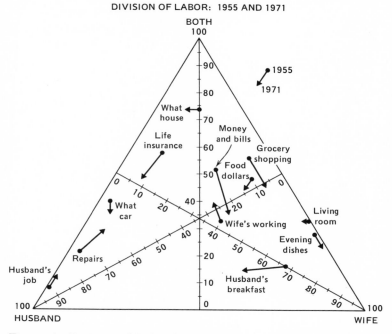

Figure 1. Division of Labor between Spouses: 1955 and 1971

larly represents a gain for "wife always"; and a shift toward the apex means that the task is more frequently shared (that is, it falls in one of the three middle categories of the distribution) in 1971 than in 1955. The first observation suggested by this display is that the general pattern of the division of labor remains intact, despite changes in the particular items. Three functions—straightening the living room, doing the dishes, and getting breakfast—remain predominantly the wife's. Four functions are done either by both spouses or by the wife primarily: grocery shopping, deciding on the food budget, taking care of the money and bills, and deciding whether the wife should work. Five items fall heavily to the husband, or are shared by both spouses but rarely are assigned to the wife primarily. These include decisions about the house, the car, life insurance, and the husband's job, and the task of doing household repairs. This classification is as clear in the 1971 statistics as it is in the 1955 data.

Another way to look at the organization of household functions is to consider the tasks two at a time. Thus, as mentioned previously, doing the evening dishes and straightening up the living room typically are tasks done by the wife alone. But is there any linkage between the two tasks apart from this similarity in their distribution? The answer is affirmative, for if husbands do assume part of the responsibility for one of these tasks they are more likely to do the same for the other. We find that there was no change in the degree to which these two tasks go together, in this sense, between 1955 and 1971. The same analysis was carried out for each of the 66 ($= 12 \times 11/2$) pairs of tasks, but we shall not present the statistical results in detail. For almost all pairs of tasks there is some association. For the bulk of them, as was true in the example given, the association remained the same in 1971 as in 1955. In only 7 of the 66 pairs of tasks was there any change in this association, and 5 of the 7 pertain to the one item, who decides on how much money to spend for food. As we observed, this decision in 1971 was assigned to the husband more often than in 1955, although it remains primarily in the wife's domain or a shared decision. For reasons that are not entirely clear, the association of this decision with grocery shopping, getting breakfast, doing dishes, taking care of the money and bills, and deciding on what house to take has changed, at least to a statistically significant degree. If we had more information about how couples work out the entire household budget, we might better understand why this particular decision seems to have a somewhat unstable relationship to several other tasks and decisions. But the main finding is worth re-emphasizing: Most tasks and decisions do have a stable pattern of association with other items of the division of labor, and in that sense the organization of functions in the household has undergone relatively little change since the 1950s.

Women and Work

The rapid change in the frequency of women working out-side the home is widely recognized. The trend may be sum-marized by noting that 21 percent of married women living with their husbands were in the labor force in 1950 as compared with 35 percent in 1970, according to U.S. Census data for the three-county Detroit metropolitan area. There continues to be lively discussion in the mass media regarding the questions of whether, or under what circum-stances, women should work, and of the reasons why they may want to work.

Our material does not relate to the factors that directly determine women's decisions on this matter, but to the general climate of opinion on the subject. No doubt women are sensitive to such opinion. At least, on the evidence given earlier, we can be sure that they are aware of their hus-bands' views. Three-fifths of the wives interviewed in 1955 and two-thirds of those interviewed in 1971 stated that their decision about working either was shared in some measure with the husband or was actually left to him en-tirely (Table 5).

To gauge the general drift of opinion on women's work, we used a set of questions concerning reasons why women work—as the respondent, male or female, inter-prets them—and whether women have special problems in working or whether there are particular kinds of work they should not undertake.[1] Two of the questions were open-ended; that is, the respondent was asked to state her or his opinion in her or his own words. The answers obtained were coded into the categories used in Tables 6 and 8. To be sure that the 1956 and 1971 data would be comparable, the 1956 interviews were recoded by the same staff that coded the 1971 interviews. This precaution was well ad-vised, for it turned out that the 1971 coders interpreted the

[1] See Detroit Area Study, *A Social Profile of Detroit, 1956* (Ann Arbor: University of Michigan, 1957), Chapter 4, "Women in the Labor Force."

21

same material from the 1956 interviews differently from the original (1956) coders. This happened often enough, at least, to have rendered estimates of change equivocal if we had not made the extra effort to assure comparability.

The primacy of money among the reasons why women are thought to work is unchanged between 1956 and 1971. In both years, 89 percent of the respondents mentioned money; and 55 percent mentioned no reason other than the need or desire for money. Mentions of money appear as frequently in the answers of men as in the answers of women (see Table 6). Their shared view of the importance of money is, moreover, in general accord with the reports of women in a national survey who took jobs during 1963: half said they went to work because of economic necessity, another sixth to earn extra money.[2]

The most frequently mentioned noneconomic reason for women working is variously described as a desire to get out of the house, boredom at home, or a dislike of housework or married life. Mentions of the desire to get out of the house increased in frequency between 1956 and 1971 and also appear more often in the answers of women than in the answers of men. The increase here seems to reflect a growing recognition by men of women's reasons, rather than a growing restlessness on the part of women. Female respondents did not change their views on why most women work between 1956 and 1971; the males became more likely to mention women's desire to get out of the house. (Other changes in Table 6 are so small that they may represent only sampling error.)

Although a decisive majority of respondents continued to feel that women have special problems working, the opinion was held less widely in 1971 than in 1956. When asked if women had special problems, 73 percent of the

[2] Another sixth said the most important reason was either completion of schooling or a job offer; the remaining sixth cited personal satisfaction. Carl Rosenfeld and Vera C. Perrella, "Why Women Start and Stop Working: A Study of Mobility," *Special Labor Force Report*, No. 59, reprinted from *Monthly Labor Review*, September 1965, Bureau of Labor Statistics, U.S. Department of Labor, Table A.

Table 6. Opinions on Why Women Work

Why do you think most women work?	Percent Distribution					
	Total		Women		Men	
	1956	1971	1956	1971	1956	1971
(Reasons mentioned)						
Money only	56	55	54	54	58	56
Money and also another reason	33	34	33	35	33	33
To get out of the house	11	14	14	16	7	12
To keep busy	6	5	6	4	6	5
To be independent	5	4	4	3	7	5
The work itself	4	5	3	5	4	5
Some other reason	7	6	6	7	9	6
Only reasons other than money	11	11	13	11	9	11
	100	100	100	100	100	100

1956 respondents answered yes; by comparison, in 1971 65 percent of the respondents answered yes. In neither year did men answer yes more often than women (see Table 7).

Those respondents—both male and female—who felt that women had special problems working were somewhat more likely to feel that women should not have certain kinds of work. An appreciable number who held one opinion did not hold the other, however; and the association between the two opinions was looser in 1971 than in 1956.

The issue on which women and men disagree is whether there should be restrictions on the kinds of work women have. Women, whatever their view on the special problems women encounter in working, opposed restrictions on the work women can do more often than did their male counterparts. The disagreement has persisted although a significant shift in opinion from a restrictive toward a nonrestrictive position occurred between 1956 and 1971 among both males and females.

Even among women interviewed in 1971, the majority sentiment held that women should not have certain

Table 7. Opinions on Women's Problems in Working

Do you feel that women have special problems working? Are there some kinds of work that you feel women should not have?	Percent Distribution					
	Total		Women		Men	
	1956	1971	1956	1971	1956	1971
Yes (have special problems)	73	65	71	65	74	64
Yes (some work they shouldn't have)	60	45	56	42	65	48
No	13	20	15	23	9	16
No (no special problems)	27	35	29	35	26	36
Yes (some work they shouldn't have)	19	22	19	20	20	26
No	8	13	10	15	6	10
	100	100	100	100	100	100

kinds of work. The proportion voicing an objection stood at 62 percent among the 1971 female respondents. By way of comparison, the corresponding proportions were 75 percent among the 1956 female respondents, 74 percent among the 1971 male respondents, and 85 percent among the 1956 male respondents (see Table 8). The predominant theme of the objections is the physical difficulty of some work which renders it unsuitable for women.

The kinds of unsuitable work mentioned most often are factory jobs, men's jobs, and hard jobs. Among the respondents who felt that women should not have some kinds of work, fewer objected to women having jobs in factories in 1971 than had objected in 1956, and fewer of those who objected to factory jobs said they did so for any reason other than that the work was hard. The decrease in mentions of factory work was offset by an increase in mentions of men's work and hard work, however. More 1971 respondents objected to women having jobs traditionally filled by men, such as plumbing, truck driving, railroading, welding, highway work, or construction. More also objected to women having jobs which require hard labor or are performed under dirty or dangerous conditions. Changes in

Table 8. Opinions on Kinds of Work Women Should Not Have

Are there kinds of work you feel women should not have? [If yes,] What are they? Why do you feel this way?	*Percent Mention Each Reason*					
	Total		*Women*		*Men*	
	1956	*1971*	*1956*	*1971*	*1956*	*1971*
No, no work women should not have	20	33	25	38	15	26
Yes[a]	80	67	75	62	85	74
(Reasons why) Factory jobs	34	15	37	14	32	15
Too hard	10	7	11	7	9	7
Degrading	6	2	8	2	5	2
Takes jobs from men	7	2	7	2	6	2
Some other reason	11	4	11	3	12	4
Men's jobs, e.g. crafts, drivers	19	27	15	25	24	29
Too hard	8	15	7	13	11	16
Degrading	3	3	3	3	3	3
Takes jobs from men	2	1	2	1	1	1
Some other reason	6	8	3	8	9	9
Professional or administrative jobs	7	9	7	10	6	8
Not capable	4	4	5	5	3	3
Some other reason	3	5	2	5	3	5
Hard work, bad working conditions	21	32	17	26	26	39
Work not thought to be respectable	5	1	6	1	4	1
Where they take jobs from men	4	2	5	3	3	1

[a] Categories given below are not mutually exclusive so they will total to a percentage greater than those saying yes.

the response pattern of men resemble those in the response pattern of women.

Other kinds of objections were voiced by relatively few respondents either in 1956 or in 1971. Objections to women having professional or administrative jobs increased in frequency of mention over the 15-year period. Concern about the respectability of the work or the possible displacement of male workers from jobs was expressed less frequently in 1971 than in 1956. The question of respectability decreased in salience for both men and women; the decrease in mentions of displacement was concentrated among men; and the increase in objections to women having professional or administrative jobs was concentrated among women.

The single persistent difference between men and women with respect to grounds for restricting women's work is the greater salience of hard work to men. Mentions of factory jobs were somewhat more common on the part of women, and mentions of traditionally male jobs more common on the part of men in 1956; but the sex differentials were absent in 1971. Two sex differentials emerged, however: in 1971 women were more likely than men to say that high prestige jobs, the professions and decision-making positions, were unsuitable for women, and to express concern about the possibility of displacing men from jobs.

Each aspect of women's work investigated—the reasons for working, the special problems encountered, and the kinds of work felt to be unsuitable—shows a distinctive pattern of temporal change and sex linkage. Stability over time and a general consensus between women and men characterize opinions as to why women work. A decrease over time and continued consensus between the sexes characterize attitudes about the presence of special problems for the working woman. A decrease over time and a persistent sex difference characterize attitudes about the unsuitability of some kinds of work for women.

Rearing Children

How children grow up is significant for social change in two ways. First, social changes affecting family, neighborhood, community, school, and other institutions may induce changes in the way children are raised and the impact of their environment on them. Hence, one would be interested in the effects of other changes on child rearing. Second, if we know something about changes in the ways children grow up, we may have some basis for anticipating future change in the adult world, for today's children are tomorrow's citizens. Thus, changes in child rearing may precipitate other changes. Although these concerns amply justify an inquiry into changes in child rearing, in this report we shall not be able to establish with any certainty the causal relationship in either direction. Our interpretations, as is true for other topics as well, include much speculation.

Most of our material relates to the base-line study, conducted in 1953, in which mothers of children under 19 years of age were the respondents. It happens that our study comes just eighteen years later, so that the children whose behavior is described in the 1971 data are the immediate successors of those whose mothers reported on them in 1953. Many of the latter, of course, were old enough to have been respondents in their own right in the 1971 survey, so that the children of 1953 appear as the young adults of 1971. To the extent that child rearing practices are related to later adult behavior, the data on the 1953 children might have forecast something about what today's young adults would be like—if only we knew how to make the appropriate inferences—while the 1971 data may have something to tell us about changes in the behavior of young adults from 1971 to 1989. Unfortunately, we do not yet understand the connections between how children are reared and what they are like as adults well enough to undertake an exercise in social forecasting. But we may suppose that if social scientists ever do realize some part of their age-old ambition to foretell the future, they will require better information than has been available thus far on changes in upbringing. In the original presentation of the 1953 study, Miller and Swanson noted the lack of data on trends in child care and suggested that part of their task was to "provide benchmarks against which future investigators can match their own results," inasmuch as "a superior way to study change is to take periodic samples from the stream of history."[1] We concur in this judgment and applaud their foresight in anticipating replications of their research.

We used only a few of Miller and Swanson's questions, but usually followed their procedure of asking them of mothers only. Some of the questions concern general norms, goals, and methods of rearing children without special reference to a particular child. Others are phrased so as to refer to a specific child. In both the 1953 and 1971 surveys, if there were two or more eligible children, the specific child was selected at random from the list of all children (under 19 years of age) of the respondent in the household roster. Although the selection was random, the probabilities of selection varied according to the order in which children were listed in the roster, and this order was not the same in the two studies. For this reason, a larger proportion of the selected children in the 1971 study are female, so that we standardize the comparisons for sex of selected child where necessary.

SEX DIFFERENTIATION OF CHORES

If changes in children's sex roles should turn out to be prognostic of changes in adult sex roles, the data in Table 9 would seem to forecast future changes in the division of labor by sex, as previously described in Tables 4 and 5. When mothers report what chores are suited to performance by an adolescent boy, girl, or both, they tend to

---

[1] Daniel R. Miller and Guy E. Swanson, *The Changing American Parent*, New York: Wiley, 1958, p. 216.

acknowledge in the aggregate that some tasks are more appropriately assigned to boys, and others to girls. But the degree to which traditions of sex specialization are respected has decreased considerably. For the two illustrative tasks that, in the past, would usually have been assigned to a boy and also the two that would have been done by a girl, there was an increase in the proportion of mothers stating that the task should regularly be done by both boys and girls. Indeed, for two of the tasks—washing the car and making beds—the "unisex" approach is the preponderant choice now, though it was endorsed by a minority of mothers in 1953. A third task, shoveling walks, is now seen as suitable for both sexes by just half the mothers, although only one-third of the 1953 mothers felt this way. The one task that shows only a modest change (not statistically significant) in this direction is dusting furniture.

It is interesting that there is no tendency in these data for an exchange of sex roles between boys and girls. That is, in 1971 there were no more mothers who would, with seeming perversity, assign car washing to a girl in preference to a boy. Rather, the entirety of the change has been toward the elimination of sex as a criterion for allo-

Table 9. Sex Differentiation of Chores

Here are some things that might be done by a boy or a girl. Suppose the person were about 13 years old. As I read each of these to you, I would like you to tell me if it should be done as a regular task by a boy, by a girl, or by both.		*Percent Distribution of Mothers*				
		Boy	*Girl*	*Both*	*Neither*	*Total*
Shoveling walks	1953	65	0	34	1	100
	1971	50	0	50	<1	100
Washing the car	1953	65	<1	29	6	100
	1971	30	<1	69	1	100
Dusting furniture	1953	1	66	32	1	100
	1971	<1	62	37	<1	100
Making beds	1953	1	52	46	1	100
	1971	<1	29	71	<1	100

cation of children's household tasks. If we had a wider range of illustrative tasks, or other data indicative of sex role differentiation, it might be possible to determine which kind of change mothers are more willing to make—to let girls do what used to be boys' jobs, or to let boys do what used to be girls' jobs. However, it appears from Table 9 that we cannot easily generalize on this matter, since the changes for the four items are at quite different rates. Even so, in 1971 the items remain associated, each with every one of the remaining three, in much the same pattern that they were in 1953 (except that the association of sex specialization in shoveling walks with sex specialization in washing the car is somewhat stronger in the later year). Thus, if mothers favor a sexual basis for division of labor among children in regard to one task, they are likely to do so with respect to another, and this remains true in 1971 as it was in 1953, even though fewer mothers now endorse sex specialization.

AGE NORMS

Recent events have sensitized us to changes in age roles as well as sex roles. The lowering of the legal age of adulthood from 21 to 18 may perhaps be seen as an adaptation to the scientifically established fact that biological maturation occurs at an earlier age than was true in the past. Moreover, we know that children encounter formal agencies of socialization—the kindergarten, nursery school, and child care centers—at early ages far more often than they did even a few years ago. Finally, the youngsters under 19 reported on in this study nearly all grew up under the watchful eye of the television tube and hardly escaped acquiring from it a certain precocious sophistication. Counter to these trends of making children into adults sooner, there is, of course, the extension of schooling through high school graduation for the majority and through college for a large fraction of recent cohorts—a prolongation of childhood, in a sense.

Parents are, of course, attentive to social norms concerning appropriate behavior and expected skills of children in relation to their age; the "child development" literature has been popular in some circles during the life time of the children whose rearing is under examination here. No doubt this fact is well known to all who have heard of Dr. Spock and his predecessors or successors. We have statistical evidence from the question, "Have there been times in the last month when you've wanted to find out what behavior to expect from children at a particular age, or about how to get children to do something?" In 1953, a small majority of mothers, 54 percent, answered yes; by coincidence, the same majority of 54 percent replied affirmatively in 1971. We infer that parental concern with these matters is about the same now as it was two decades ago.

We have data on four specific kinds of behavior that may be expected of children. Mothers were asked: "Here are some tasks that some parents require of their children. Which of these did you or would you require of [selected child's name] and by what age?" Picking up his or her own toys is a task that most mothers expect to be performed before the child reaches school age, the most frequent ages given by the mothers being 2 or 3. The cumulative age distributions (Figure 2) constructed from the 1953 and 1971 data are quite similar. There is, however, a very small though significant shift toward a higher age for this task. The median age was 3 years, 2 months in 1953; in 1971 it was 3 years, 5 months. The shift arises primarily from a decrease in the frequency of mothers expecting the child to pick up toys before reaching the second birthday.

The age norm is not quite so sharply defined for putting away one's own clothes (Figure 2). The most frequent ages are 4 and 5. The cumulative distributions again show a small upward shift owing, in particular, to the decrease in proportion of mothers expecting this performance at a very early age. The median registers a change from 4 years, 11 months in 1953 to 5 years, 5 months in 1971, or an increase of half a year in the age at which the average child is expected to put away his or her own clothes.

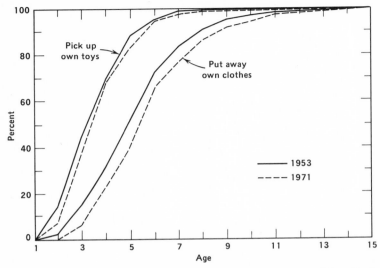

Figure 2. Percent of Mothers Who Would Require Child to Pick Up His/Her Own Toys and Percent Who Would Require Child to Put Away His/Her Own Clothes by a Given Age or Younger. (Unweighted average of cumulative distributions for male and female children.)

The age distribution for the task of dressing oneself is very much like that for picking up toys, except that it comes two years later in the life cycle. Between 1953 and 1971 there was a slight increase in the proportion of children expected to dress themselves at the atypically young age of 2 or 3. But the remainder of the two distributions are closely similar (Figure 3). The median age in the two years was just the same: 5 years, 3 months.

The most dramatic changes occurred for the task of running errands to a nearby store. In 1953, one out of eight mothers expected this before the child reached school age, but only one in forty of the 1971 mothers did so. There were also upward shifts in the remainder of the distribution (Figure 3). In 1971 there was less consensus among mothers as to the appropriate age for this activity; that is, the age norm had become less sharply defined. The median

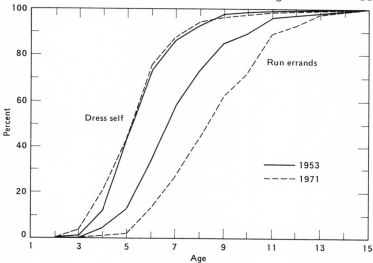

Figure 3. Percent of Mothers Who Would Require Child to Dress Himself/Herself Completely, and Percent Who Would Require Him/Her to Run Errands to Nearby Store by a Given Age or Younger. (Unweighted average of cumulative distributions for male and female children.)

age increased from 6 years, 8 months in 1953 to 8 years, 4 months in 1971. It is hard to believe that this change can be due to a drastic alteration in parents' perceptions of the capabilities of their children, especially in the face of the rather small changes (albeit in the same direction) for two of the other three tasks. It would seem that we must look to the child's environment for an explanation of this change. Perhaps the "nearby store" is not so "nearby" in 1971 as it was in 1953. It may have turned into a supermarket many blocks or several miles away. In both years, running errands was expected of boys earlier than girls, the difference in median ages being about half a year. This suggests that one consideration in determining when to require this task of the child is the mother's feeling about her or his safety on the street. It is, of course, only a conjecture that more mothers had misgivings on this score in

1971 than in 1953 and adjusted their expectations of their children accordingly. For whatever cause, we have in the instance of this task a very marked counter current to the trends, mentioned before, that appear to be conferring adult responsibilities at an earlier age.

The same observation applies to data on a broader question pertaining to the age to which a mother should supervise the child's activity (Table 10). Statistically, there is no question about the substantial increase in the age distribution between 1953 and 1971. The finding does invite speculation as to the causes of the shift. However, no unambiguous interpretation seems possible, for the question itself is fatally ambiguous. Symptomatically, many respondents indicated that the question was difficult to answer, that the answer depends on how one interprets "supervision," and that particular circumstances—for example, whether the child is in school—would govern the decision in particular cases. Moreover, the age distributions are too spread out and irregular for us to assume that all mothers attached the same meaning to the question. For what it is worth, therefore, we merely report that many

Table 10. Age to Which Supervision Is Needed

Some mothers believe that for a child's own good they should know what (he/she) is doing most of the time and should supervise (him/her) until a certain age. What age would you say that should be?	Percent Distribution[a] of Mothers	
	1953	1971
Before 5 years	9	1
5 to 8 years	21	12
9 to 12 years	12	13
13 to 15 years	17	12
16 or 17 years	11	17
18 to 20 years	17	29
21 years or older	4	5
As long as living in parents' house	9	11
	100	100

[a] Unweighted average of distributions for male and female children.

more mothers in 1971 than in 1953 felt that the child should be "supervised" to an age that the law now regards as adult. We regret that this tantalizing result and its equivocal meaning were not anticipated, so that we cannot offer even a tentative interpretation.

PARENTAL RESPONSE

We turn from the specification of sex and age norms for the child's behavior to the mother's response when these or other expectations are violated by the child. Asked how to handle a crying infant, if she/he were only crying to get attention, two-fifths of the mothers in both 1953 and 1971 responded that they would do nothing but let the child cry (Table 11). What did change was the relative popularity of two other kinds of actions recognized in the codes for this open question: to do something immediately or regardless of why the child was crying, or to let what she decides to do depend on other factors in the situation, thus sometimes delaying any response to the child's crying. The former alternative gained considerably at the expense of the latter. Miller and Swanson present this question as one of their "internalization indices," reasoning that a mother who does nothing for a crying child or delays

Table 11. Response to Baby's Crying

Mothers have different ways of handling a crying child of five months. Suppose that you were busy preparing the family dinner and the baby was cranky and crying—if you thought nothing was wrong with (him/her), and (he/she) only wanted attention, what would you do?	Percent Distribution of Mothers	
	1953	1971
1. Immediate or unconditional action	35	44
2. Do nothing, let child cry	41	41
3. Other (delayed or conditional action; check if child is all right; sometimes let him cry; sometimes do something; someone else would do something)	24	15
	100	100

giving him or her any attention may be seeking to encourage the habit of self-control or self-denial. These authors recognize, of course, that the same action might be taken for different reasons by different mothers. But, if this interpretation of the question is generally appropriate, we should have to conclude that mothers today are less interested in inculcating self-control than were mothers in 1953.

This conclusion must be accepted with caution, however. Much depends on whether the coders of the 1971 open-ended question interpreted the codes in the same way as the 1953 coders. A thorough study of this matter could not be made, as we were able to recover only four-fifths of the 1953 questionnaires. (The missing ones, however, were apparently removed at random from the file.) After the 1971 coders recoded the 1953 responses, we could make rough corrections to the 1953 distributions. We do not show revised 1953 figures, as we do not have great confidence in the quality of the estimated corrections. But we can indicate the direction and order of magnitude of the probable bias in the 1953 distributions relative to those for 1971 where there are significant differences between the two teams of coders. In the instance of Table 11, it appears that recoding does not affect the finding of "no change" in the percentage of mothers who would "do nothing." However, the frequency of "immediate action" is probably understated and that of "other" is overstated in the uncorrected 1953 figures. Hence, the change as portrayed by Table 11 is exaggerated and may not even be statistically significant.

Two more of Miller and Swanson's internalization indices are examined in the next two tables. A parent bent on inculcating self-control, it is supposed, will more frequently resort to symbolic rewards for good behavior or symbolic punishments for bad behavior than will a parent not preoccupied with this objective in child rearing. Whatever the reason—including probable noncomparability of coding—there are significant shifts in the frequency with which certain kinds of reward are mentioned (Table 12). The most striking change is the increase from 1 percent to 18 percent of mothers mentioning the display of overt affec-

Table 12. Rewards for Good Behavior

Think about a time when [name of child] (will be/ was) ten years old. (He/She) has just done something that you feel is very good, or (he/she) has been particularly good. What would you do at those times?	*Percent Mention*[a]	
	1953	*1971*
1. Psychic reward: satisfactions expected to come from within the child for a job well-done (e.g. mother tells him he should feel good about it)	8	1
2. Other verbal praise	67	78
3. Special privileges or freedoms	13	11[b]
4. Material reward: money or gifts— concrete rewards	35	26
5. Love him, kiss him, overt affection	1	18
6. Does something, what not stated	2	<1
7. Doesn't do anything	3	1[b]

[a] Sum of percentages exceeds 100 because some respondents mentioned two rewards.

[b] Difference between years not significant.

tion as a means of rewarding the child. There is a concomitant, though not as large, decrease in the proportion mentioning some kind of concrete reward, such as money or a gift. Upon recoding, it appears that most of the apparent decrease in "psychic reward" is indeed due to noncomparability of coding. Moreover, the 1971 coders found a good deal more reference to "overt affection" in the 1953 interviews than did the 1953 coders, so that the amount of increase for this category in Table 12 is overstated, even though the direction of change in probably indicated correctly. Altogether, if the 1953 data were fully comparable to the 1971 data, the changes would probably not be great; but apparently there was some real increase in the use of verbal praise and overt affection and correlative decrease in the use of material rewards.

As to punishments, we must again discount the apparent trends in Table 13. A good deal of what the 1953 coders thought belonged under "verbal admonition" was seen by the 1971 coders as a denial by the mother that she would resort to punishment. Many responses that the 1953

Table 13. Punishments for Wrong Behavior

Now, please think about that same time when [name of child] (will be/was) ten years old. (He/She) has just done something that you feel is very wrong, something that you have warned (him/her) against ever doing. What would you do at such times?	Percent Mention[a]	
	1953	1971
1. Psychic punishment: mentions specifically that guilt or shame feelings engendered in child	3	1
2. Verbal admonitions: scoldings, warnings, or threats (excluding shame, guilt)	28	18
3. Physical punishment	31	34[b]
4. Restriction of behavior and withdrawal of privileges (kept home, no T.V., etc.)	64	59[b]
5. Would not punish, do something positive (reassure, etc.)	3	22
6. Punish, not further specified	1	2[b]
7. Do something, what not stated	2	<1

[a] Sum of percentages exceeds 100 because some respondents mentioned two different punishments.
[b] Difference between years not significant.

coders put in category 2 of Table 13 were put into category 5 by our 1971 coders. Thus, the apparent decrease in the use of verbal admonitions is spurious and the apparent spectacular increase in the resort to reassurance, etc. in lieu of punishment probably is likewise spurious. In fact, once we take account of the apparent biases of the 1953 coders, relative to those who classified the responses in 1971, it becomes doubtful whether there really were any significant changes in the distribution of responses to the question on punishment.

One might justifiably raise the question of why two groups of coders would see the same material in such a different light. We think it is likely that the 1953 coders were carefully trained by Miller and Swanson to appreciate certain rather subtle conceptual distinctions that are not adequately conveyed by the brief descriptions of the code categories, whereas these descriptions were all our 1971 coders had to go on· In retrospect, it also appears that the earlier investigators would have been well advised to code only the

manifest content of the responses and to develop such interpretations as "psychic reward" and "psychic punishment"
in the course of the analysis, rather than in the coding
process. In any event, we are warned here, as at one or two
other places in the study, that inferences about change are
most precarious when there is a serious likelihood of failure
in comparability of study procedures. Fortunately, most of
our material on childrearing does not seem to have incurred
this problem. For the topic of parental response to child's
behavior, however, we must conclude that the changes, if
any, were small relative to the errors created by discrepancies in understanding and application of the code categories.

AUTONOMY OF THE CHILD

A final group of questions may be characterized
roughly as bearing in one way or another upon the child's
autonomy, or the extent to which parents and others believe a child should be encouraged to find his own solutions
to problems. In the early 1950s there was much talk of
recent tendencies for Americans to become "other-directed,"
that is, more responsive to the feelings, responses, and
expectations of persons in their social milieu and less so
to their own sense of what is right or valuable. In the somewhat hypothetical question put to mothers in 1953 which
seemingly invited them to make a choice between inner-
directedness and other-directedness for their child, Miller
and Swanson found that a few more than half chose the
inner-directed alternative, a third the other-directed alternative, and a seventh some mixture or qualification of
these two alternatives. It could not, of course, be deter-
mined at that time whether 33 percent was a high or low
proportion of other-directed answers, relative to historical
experience. What we can say now, however, given the data
in Table 14, is that if there was a trend toward other-
directedness prior to 1953, it has since been reversed. In
1971, only one-tenth of the mothers said that a child should
be encouraged to change his activities if that were neces-

Table 14. Preference for Inner-Directed or Other-Directed
Activities

	Percent Distribution of Mothers	
Suppose a 14-year-old child were interested in some worthwhile activities that gave (him/her) little time to spend with other children. The things the other children are doing are just as worthwhile, but they don't interest this particular child. Would you encourage (him/her) in going on with (his/her) own interests, or would you rather see (him/her) change to something (he/she) can do with other children?	1953	1971
1. Continue with own interests	53	73
2. Be with others	33	10
3. Mixed or qualified answers	14	17
	100	100

sary in order for him to do things with other children. Almost three-quarters stated that he should continue with his own interests, even if such interests do not lead him to associate with others.

A somewhat different facet of the child's autonomy is the extent to which he is allowed by parents to make his own decisions. In the 1958 survey, parents were asked, "Do you feel that a twelve-year old should be allowed to decide for himself whether he will go to church or Sunday School, or should his parents decide this?" About one-sixth (17 percent) of all mothers and fathers (without regard to the current age of their children) said that the child should decide. In the 1971 survey, we found that the fraction had risen above one-fifth (22 percent). There is some uncertainty in the result, since we cannot precisely identify fathers, all of whose children have left home, among the 1971 male respondents. The direction of the change, nevertheless, does not seem to be in doubt even though it is not a very large change.

In a secular and somewhat broader context, we have interesting evidence that the issue of autonomy can reveal pronounced cleavages in the population. In Table 15 we have delineated a "cohort chasm" in showing responses to

Table 15. Cohort Chasm and Generation Gap

Which statement do you agree more with?
—The younger generation should be taught by their elders to do what is right.
—The younger generation should be taught to think for themselves even though they may do something their elders disapprove of.
How do you think your (father/mother) [parent of same sex as respondent] would have answered this question when you were growing up? Which one would (he/she) have agreed with more [1971 only]?

Respondent's Age	Percent "Do Right"		
	1956	*1971*	*1971 Parents*
Under 35[a]	47	34	73
35[a]–49	49	48	82
50–64	66	64	93
65–79	} 75	79	95
80 and over		79	100
All Ages	54	50	83

[a] Under 36 and 36–49 in 1971 data.

a question about the desirability of autonomy in the "younger generation" by fifteen-year age intervals. In both 1956 and 1971, younger adults saw the matter quite differently from older adults, the latter feeling that the younger generation should be taught to do what is right and the former more often stating that the younger generation should be taught to think for themselves. For the aggregate of all age groups, in the fifteen-year period between the two surveys, there was only a slight decline, from 54 to 50 percent, in the popularity of the do right alternative —too slight, in fact, to be recorded as statistically significant in the absence of cross-classification by other variables. Reading the table across its rows, we see that for each of the age groups above 35 there was little change in the percentages favoring each alternative. But for respondents under 35, there was a sharp decline, from 47 percent saying do right in 1956 to 34 percent preferring this alternative in 1971.

Another perspective on these data is secured by comparing the 1956 figure for each age group with the 1971 figure for the next older group. In this way, we can trace the change as recorded in two observations, spaced fifteen years apart, on each cohort (except, of course, those under 35 in 1971). We find that the pattern of intracohort change is much like what we would have expected from the 1956 pattern of age differences. Thus, aging from 35–49 (in 1956) to 50–64 (in 1971) was accompanied by an increase from 49 to 64 percent favoring the do right alternative. The cohort under 35 in 1956 scarcely changed its division of opinion on the question over the fifteen year period, as one might have anticipated from their similarity to the cohort 35–49 years old in the earlier year. What could not have been forecast from the 1956 age pattern, however, is the marked drop in percentage saying do right among the youngest cohort in 1971, as compared to its counterpart of 1956. Although there is no way in which this might have been foreseen from the 1956 data, perhaps this finding contains a clue as to what we might foresee in the data for 1986, if there should be another survey then. If the youngest cohort in 1971 follows the pattern of its predecessors, it will not change its percentage in the next fifteen years. In that event, the 35–49 group in 1986 will show a drop as compared with the same age group in 1971 (or 1956). Moreover, if the new cohort, under 35 in 1986, shows the same kind of shift as its predecessor at the same age, there will be an even lower percentage to enter in the first row of the 1986 column.

Our aim is not to offer a serious forecast, but to illustrate how the process of social metabolism—the replacement of one cohort by its successor—may be combined with the process of aging, which here seems to induce a conservative view on the question at issue, to produce the social change that we observe on an aggregate basis. Of course, our clues as to how this is working in the present instance are not infallible, and it would be easy to suggest other configurations of forces that would produce the contrasts among age groups observed in the data for these two years. The contrasts themselves are unmistakable: people differing in age see this matter in different perspectives.

The "generation gap," properly understood, refers not to the contrast between people of different ages—although the term is popularly used in this sense—but, precisely, to the difference between people who are related as one generation to another, i.e., parents to their offspring, or a subpopulation however defined to their parents. Of course, parents are older than their children, but the parent-offspring age difference is by no means a constant. Hence, we can never accurately infer the extent of a generation gap from comparisons of age groups. The data in Table 15 suggest, moreover, that offspring (the respondents in the 1971 survey) *see* the generation gap as much more pronounced than the actual differences probably are. This is no doubt a matter of selective perception, but such selectivity is surely part of the gap, by its very nature. Interestingly, every cohort represented in this population reports the parental generation as being much more conservative than itself. Hence, the generation gap can hardly be a recent invention.

A final question on general goals in rearing children, as seen by the whole adult population, touches in part on the same theme of children thinking for themselves; but it introduces other goals as well:

> If you had to choose, which thing on this list would you pick as the most important for a child to learn to prepare him for life?
> [A] To obey
> [B] To be well liked or popular
> [C] To think for himself
> [D] To work hard
> [E] To help others when they need help
> Which comes next? Which comes third? Which is fourth [In 1958: Which is least important]?

Respondents answering all four questions in a consistent way provided, in effect, a preference ordering of the five

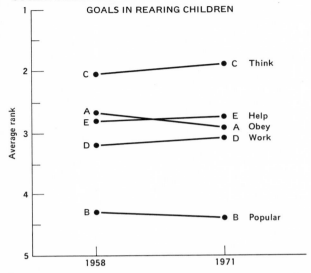

Figure 4. Average Ranks of Five Goals in Rearing Children

alternatives. One way to summarize the results, therefore, is to calculate the average rank of each of the five goals. The comparison of the averages in Figure 4 suggests a generally stable value pattern, but also reveals some significant shifts. The goals of learning obedience and how to be well liked became less desirable in 1971 than they were in 1958, relative to the goals of thinking for oneself, helping others, and working hard. Indeed, to obey fell from second to third place in terms of average rank, being overtaken by help others. Within the two groups, [A] and [B] vs [C], [D], and [E], there was no significant shift, that is, of obey with respect to popular, or of think, help, and work with respect to one another. On the whole, our findings with this question seem consistent with the decline in emphasis on "other-directedness" reported earlier. But the decreasing importance of being well liked does not necessarily imply approval of complete detachment from others, for "to help others" went up as much as "to be well liked or popular" went down.

Social Participation

The idea of informal social participation that was communicated to our respondents is contained in the wording of the question: "We are also interested in how Detroiters spend their spare time. Many people get together every once in a while to visit, or play cards, or do something else. How often do you usually get together with any of your relatives other than those living at home with you?" Beginning with, "How often . . . ," the question was repeated for "any of your neighbors," "outside of work with any people you (or your husband) work(ed) with," and "any other friends who are not neighbors or fellow workers." The same wordings were used in the 1971 and 1959 surveys. In 1957, only the preamble was slightly different: "Apart from organizations and clubs, some people get together. . . ." In all three surveys respondents were given a card listing eight possible frequencies, ranging from (1.) Every day to (8.) Never, and asked to choose one. In Table 16 some of the eight categories have been combined.

Minor differences between the frequency distributions for 1957 and 1971 (Wayne County only) and 1959 and 1971 can be seen in the table. Perhaps a few of these would show statistical significance if subjected to a formal test. However, in this instance we are disinclined to emphasize the outcome of such tests in view of the fact that the 1957–71 differences are often in the opposite direction from the 1959–71 differences. Hence, it would seem that even if there are significant differences, they cannot be regarded as estimates of a long-term trend. The most succinct summary seems to be that there is no evidence for a trend toward increasing or decreasing informal participation in any of the four types of participation included in the table. One is impressed, on the contrary, with the apparent stability in the patterns.

Another piece of evidence to this effect derives from the question, "In general, would you say that the people in your neighborhood keep pretty much to themselves, or do

Table 16. Informal Social Participation

Frequency of getting together with—	Percent Distribution			
	1957[a]	1971[a]	1959	1971
Relatives (other than those living at home with you):				
Every day; or almost every day	4	7	7	6
Once or twice a week	32	31	35	31
A few times a month	20	20	21	20
Once a month	12	13	12	14
A few times a year	17	20	14	20
Less often	6	5	4	5
Never	9	4	7	4
	100	100	100	100
Neighbors:				
Every day; or almost every day	10	13	13	12
Once or twice a week	18	16	19	17
A few times a month; or once a month	18	19	23	20
A few times a year; or less often	19	22	22	23
Never	35	30	23	28
	100	100	100	100
People you or your husband work with:				
Once or twice a week; or more often	17	15	15	14
A few times a month; or once a month	22	24	22	24
A few times a year; or less often	30	33	36	34
Never	31	28	27	28
	100	100	100	100
Friends who are not neighbors or fellow workers:				
Once or twice a week; or more often	28	29	25	29
A few times a month; or once a month	38	35	37	36
A few times a year; or less often	23	28	29	28
Never	11	8	9	7
	100	100	100	100

[a] Wayne County only.

they get together quite a bit?" In the 1957 survey, 77 percent replied that people keep to themselves. Again in the 1971 survey (Wayne County only, for comparability), 77 percent gave this answer.

Apart from the interest in the finding of stability in its own right, there is the important implication from these results that other social changes can hardly be explained by changes in the pattern of informal relations among people, given that the latter are so slight. Sociologists have produced evidence and arguments for rather pervasive effects of informal social relations—on morale, on political involvement and socialization, and many other phenomena. But, if we find changes in these phenomena, it appears that we shall have to look to sources other than the modification of the fabric of informal social participation for the causes.

Formal participation was measured in 1959 and 1971 by providing the respondent with a list of kinds of organizations, asking him which of these kinds he belongs to, and whether he usually attends meetings of this group at least once a month. It seems expedient to classify the responses by sex of respondent, since some of the organizations recruit mainly men as members and some mainly women.

In terms of the percentages of men and women belonging to organizations of different kinds, rather few significant changes are shown in Table 17. Men reported increasing membership in sports teams and decreasing membership in neighborhood improvement associations. Women reported decreases in organizations based on nationality and veteran's organizations. Both men and women showed a substantial drop in the frequency of membership in church-connected groups. This is especially striking since this category has the highest membership frequency for women and for men is second only to unions. Some caution must be exercised in the interpretation of this result. Other evidence on religion, reported subsequently, suggests that the 1959 survey secured atypically high levels of church attendance and other manifestations of interest in religious matters. We are uncertain whether this is due to special features of this particular survey and is thus, in

Table 17. Association Membership, by Type

Memberships in Clubs or Organizations of Specified Kinds:	Percent Belonging					
	Total		Men		Women	
	1959	1971	1959	1971	1959	1971
Labor unions	28	27	47	45	9	12
Church-connected groups	36	28[a]	30	24[a]	42	31[a]
Fraternal organizations or lodges	14	12	19	17	10	8
Veteran's organizations	6	5	9	11	3	<1[a]
Business or civic groups	5	7	7	10	3	4
Parent-teacher associations	19	20	12	13	25	26
Neighborhood clubs or community centers	8	10	7	9	8	10
Organizations of people of the same nationality	6	4[a]	5	4	7	3[a]
Sport teams	11	15[a]	13	21[a]	8	9
Professional groups	7	8	10	12	5	5
Political clubs or organizations	3	2	3	3	3	2
Neighborhood improvement associations	12	8[a]	13	9[a]	11	8
Card clubs; women's or men's social clubs	12	13	8	9	17	16
Charitable and welfare organizations	9	7	7	6	10	8

[a] Difference between years is statistically significant; other differences in the table are not.

some sense, an artifact, or whether the conditions of that particular year were especially conducive to religious participation. In either event, we should not wish to conclude that the 1959–1971 difference in memberships in church-connected groups necessarily represents a long-run trend. There is some ambiguity in the category itself, inasmuch as it does not distinguish church-connected groups with a specifically religious or devotional purpose from groups that may be organized by members of a congregation for other social purposes.

The data on attendance at meetings are not presented in Table 17, but these data likewise show few substantial changes. By way of summary, we aggregated overall categories of organization and found that 58 percent of the male members reported attendance once a month or more often in 1959, and 64 percent in 1971. Corresponding figures for women were 71 percent in 1959 and 69 percent in 1971. The 1959 figure for men is raised to 59 percent, instead of 58, when the 1959 data are standardized to have the same distribution by organizational type as was reported in 1971. For women, standardization does not affect the comparison at all.

Table 18 displays the membership data in terms of the number of different kinds of organization the respondent mentioned, of those listed in Table 17. The frequency distribution is somewhat skewed in both years, with a few respondents belonging to as many as six or eight kinds of organizations, but most reporting membership in three or fewer. The changes in the frequency distributions seem fairly minor, except that women do show a rise in the proportion reporting no memberships—no doubt a reflection of the previously mentioned drop in church-connected group memberships. The average number of memberships hardly changed for men, but dropped slightly for women. The sex differences would be essentially elimi-

Table 18. Frequency of Association Memberships

Number of Different Types of Clubs and Organizations (other than Churches) Respondent Belongs to:	*Percent Distribution*					
	Total		*Men*		*Women*	
	1959	*1971*	*1959*	*1971*	*1959*	*1971*
None	22	25	17	15	27	34
One						
Union	11	10	18	18	4	4
Other	20	20	14	17	25	22
Two	22	20	25	21	20	19
Three	13	13	14	15	12	11
Four	6	7	6	8	6	5
Five	3	3	3	3	4	3
Six	1	1	1	1	1	1
Seven	1	1	1	1	<1	<1
Eight or more	1	<1	1	1	<1	<1
Number per respondent (mean)	1.75	1.66	1.90	1.93	1.61	1.44

nated if union memberships were not counted, but the decline for women would still be in evidence.

In their important study of trends in membership in voluntary associations, Hyman and Wright point up a number of difficulties in effecting reliable and comparable measurements in this area.[1] These authors find evidence of a small increase in memberships between 1955 and 1962 as reported by national surveys, with some suggestion that the upward trend may have continued thereafter. The Detroit data do not confirm this conclusion, although our comparisons are consistent with theirs in suggesting that any change has been comparatively slight, hardly enough to represent a basic modification of the distribution of memberships in the population. Our distributions are, in fact, rather different from theirs, having been elicited in a different way. The national studies simply asked the respondent to name any groups or organizations to which he belonged, whereas the Detroit surveys provided him with a list of possible kinds of organizations. It would appear that the latter procedure serves to refresh the respondent's memory and to elicit more nearly complete reports. Another difference is that the national surveys count as one membership each group to which the respondent belongs, whereas we count only the number of categories, among the fourteen listed, in which the respondent has one or more memberships. Thus, if a man belongs to a bowling league and a swimming team, he gets credit for but one membership in "sport teams."

One other point on the problem of measurement. In 1971, though not in 1959, the questionnaire carried an explicit box instructing the interviewer to probe: "Any others?" Some 6 percent of respondents in 1971 reported a membership in this connection which was not elicited by the preceding presentation of kinds of organizations. Differences between surveys in the extent of probing can,

[1] Herbert H. Hyman and Charles R. Wright, "Trends in Voluntary Association Memberships of American Adults: Replication Based on Secondary Analysis of National Sample Surveys," *American Sociological Review*, 36 (1971): 191–206.

therefore, make an appreciable difference in the reported frequency of memberships.

To conclude, not on a methodological note but with a comment on the import of these findings, we may repeat the point offered earlier in connection with informal participation. Although there is reason to believe that formal participation is significantly linked with other kinds of social behavior, social change in other domains can hardly be explained by changes in formal participation, since the latter shows essentially a stable pattern over the time span of our measurements. By the same token, it appears that social participation is not sensitive to the several kinds of change in attitudes reported in this study. Both conclusions might require some revision if the analysis were carried out for birth cohorts or other subdivisions of the population.

Religious Participation

Some of the problems of measuring change in informal participation and membership in voluntary associations are observed again in our measurements of change in religious participation. The latter, however, seem to be on a somewhat firmer basis. Table 19 shows frequency of attendance at religious services for seven different years in the 1950s as well as 1971. The distributions are not entirely comparable for the reasons detailed in the notes to the table. However, with as many as eight observations we can make a plausible conjecture as to which differences between years reflect discontinuities in measurement and which represent real changes.

The wording of the question does seem to make a difference of a few percentage points in the proportions attending once a week and not at all. Evidently the insertion of "usually" in wording B encourages the respondent to make a more liberal estimate of the frequency of attendance than does the specific time reference in wording C ("during the last year") or the blunt "Yes" or "No" to "Do you attend?" in wording A. In the 1971 survey, we opted for wording C, so that our results are most strictly comparable to those for 1958. In comparing the 1971 with the 1958 data, we secure a smaller estimate of the amount of change than would be the case in taking any other year from 1954 through 1959 as the base year. Even so, the direction of change is unmistakable: attendance has dropped off substantially. The two categories representing most frequent attendance have decreased and the three categories for less frequent attendance have gained.

The year-to-year fluctuations in the 1950s warn us to be cautious in inferring a long-run trend from the comparison between any two years, such as 1958 and 1971. The most startling apparent change is between 1958 and 1959. The reported upward shift in attendance in this one-year period is even larger than the downward shift from 1958 to 1971. It is true that the 1958–1959 change is con-

Table 19. Frequency of Attendance at Religious Services

Percent Distribution by Frequency of Attendance

Year	Question Wording[a]	Once a week	Twice a month	Once a month	Few times a year	Never	Total
1952	A	42	17		19	21	100
1954	B	46	11	10	24	9	100
1955	B	45	12	7	24	12	100
1956	B	46	14	7	26	7	100
1957	B	47	13	10	21	9	100
1958	C	43	15	7	20	15	100
1959	B	54	10	5	23	8	100
1971	C	35	13	8	26	18	100

[a] A: Do you attend religious services? Yes_____; No_____.
   Would you say you attended religious services: About once a week; About twice a month; About once a month; A few times a year? ("No" in first part coded "Never.")

   B: About how often do you usually attend religious services? Once a week; Twice a month; Once a month; A few times a year; Never.

   C: About how often, if ever, have you attended religious services during the last year? Once a week or more; Two or three times a month; Once a month; A few times a year or less; Never.

Note: 1952 data are from "Some Social and Economic Characteristics of the Detroit Area Population, 1952," Detroit Area Study, University of Michigan, 1953. 1955 data are from unpublished tabulations of "census data" for all adults in the households surveyed, not just the wives, as is the case for other 1955 data in this report. 1957 data pertain to Wayne County only.

founded with the difference in question wording. If we compare 1959 with 1957 (Wayne County only) or 1956, however, we still find a substantial shift in a very short period of time. Our guess is that this is partly a function of the survey context. In the 1959 survey, the question on attendance at religious services followed a series of some fifty questions about religious beliefs and theological issues. These could well have put the respondent in a frame of mind that would lead him to overestimate his attendance, particularly when the question was "how often do you usually attend?" without any specific time reference. In the

1958 and 1971 surveys, the question on attendance followed a sequence of five or six questions on religious preference of the respondent, that of his father, mother, and (in 1971) spouse, and whether the father and mother were more or less religious than the respondent. The contexts for the 1958 and 1971 questions, therefore, were closely comparable.

Our tentative conclusion, then, is that there is a reliable indication of a decline in attendance at religious services between the 1950s and 1971. That the 1950s themselves may have been a period of religious revival is suggested by national data on church attendance assembled by Demerath and circumspectly interpreted by him. These data suggest some decline in attendance from the last half of the 1950s to the first half of the 1960s and, to that extent, tend to confirm the Detroit results. As Demerath points out, however, the import of the changes in attendance over time, even if reliably measured, is far from clear.[1] Certainly, it would be dangerous to extrapolate from this question to other facets of religious behavior. Fortunately, we have a few other indicators, although none that has been collected in such a systematic way as the attendance data.

In the 1959 and 1971 surveys, just after the question on attendance, respondents were asked: "Many people who are interested in religion and attend services have never actually become members of a church. Are you a member of a [respondent's preference] church, of some other church, or are you not a church member?" In 1959, 71 percent claimed to be members of their preferred church and another 1 percent to be members of some other church. In 1971, the corresponding figures were 68 and 1 percent. The apparent drop from 72 percent to 69 percent in church membership, although in the same direction as the decline in attendance, is not statistically significant. Although, on

[1] N. J. Demerath III, "Trends and Anti-trends in Religious Change," in Eleanor Bernert Sheldon and Wilbert E. Moore (eds.), *Indicators of Social Change*, New York: Russell Sage Foundation, 1968, pp. 367–368.

our previous argument, the context in the 1959 survey would presumably encourage respondents to overestimate frequency of membership, the wording of the particular question was such that the respondent was actually encouraged not to report that he was a member unless he was quite sure of the fact. Without additional data, in any case, we do not have a firm basis for asserting any trend with respect to this particular indicator.

The changes in attendance reported earlier refer, of course, to the aggregate population in each year. Over a period of time some particular individuals will be increasing their attendance, others will be decreasing, and still others will continue to attend at the same rate as before. The question reported in Table 20 asks respondents to estimate their own individual changes in attendance in the

Table 20. Change in Church Attendance

	Percent Distribution		
Would you say you attend religious services	*1958*	*1959*	*1971*
More often	24	30	18
About the same, or	39	36	30
Less often	37	34	52
	100	100	100

than you did ten or fifteen years ago?

past ten or fifteen years. In 1971, as in 1958 and 1959, we find appreciable numbers of respondents in all three categories. As compared with either base year, however, the 1971 data show fewer attending "more often" and a larger proportion attending "less often" than they did ten or fifteen years ago. For reasons discussed earlier, the appreciable difference between the 1958 and 1959 percentage distributions may well be misleading as an estimate of change. We probably obtain a more reliable estimate of long-run change by accepting 1958, rather than 1959, as the base-year for comparison with 1971. In that event, our previous conclusion as to the reality of a decline in attendance since the 1950s is strongly supported, although the meaning of that decline is not made any clearer by this confirmation.

One thing is plain, however: attendance at services is by no means synonymous with interest in religion for our respondents, although there is a positive correlation between the two. Table 21 exhibits the two slightly different questions used to elicit the respondent's feeling as to whether his interest in religion changed in the last ten

Table 21. Change in Interest in Religion

1. All things considered, do you think you are more *interested*, about as interested or less interested in religion than you were ten or fifteen years ago?

	Percent Distribution		
	1958	*1971(A)*	*1971(B)*
More	49	37	39
Same	44	38	34
Less	6	25	27
	100	100	100

2. All things considered, has your *interest in religion* grown, remained the same, or decreased over the last ten or fifteen years?

	1959	*1971(A)*	*1971(B)*
Grown	59	39	35
Same	34	40	35
Decreased	7	21	30
	100	100	100

or fifteen years. Roughly speaking, about half of the respondents in all three surveys answered the question about change in attendance in the same way that they answered either question about change in religious interest. Of the remaining half, a large majority gave a combination of answers indicating that the change in attendance did not reflect accurately the change in interest; that is, interest was said to have increased while attendance remained the same or decreased, or interest was said to have remained the same while attendance decreased.

The use of two different questions to measure change in interest was prompted by the substantial difference between the 1958 and 1959 distributions. We thought it unlikely that any real difference would be this large, but that the change in question wording and/or the difference in context between the two surveys could have affected the distributions. In the 1971 survey we sought evidence for these hypotheses by varying both wording and context. In Form A of the 1971 questionnaire, either question 1 or question 2 (as they are identified in Table 21) was asked immediately following the question on attendance at religious services. The selection of question 1 or 2 was made in advance and at random. In Form B, question 1 or 2, selected at random, was asked at a later point in the sequence of questions on religion, following not only the question on attendance, but also questions on belief in God and belief in life after death. We were, of course, unable to simulate closely the 1959 procedure of asking about change in interest after a massive sequence of questions on beliefs and theological interpretations. As it turned out, question 2 seemed to be slightly influenced by the contextual variation between Forms A and B in 1971, although question 1 was not. The two questions give roughly similar distributions of change in religious interest in the 1971 survey. But any of the 1971 distributions differs quite a bit from that obtained in either 1958 or 1959. Regardless of wording and contextual variations, therefore, we seem to have a firm indication that many more respondents in 1971 admitted a recent decrease in their interest in religion than was true in 1958 or 1959. If the 1950s were indeed a period of religious revival, then it appears that the revival crested out and was followed by a religious depression. Of course, our data do not permit a choice between this cyclical interpretation and one positing a much longer-run decrease in interest in religion dating from earlier decades of this century or from the nineteenth century.

Having noted that change in attendance and change in interest are distinct experiences for the individual, although they tend to occur together, it is perhaps pertinent to point out how the two kinds of indicators complement each other. First, both change in interest and change in attendance show the same declining trend between 1958 or 1959 and 1971. Second, the two declines are somewhat distinct. That is, allowing for the decline in interest, we still find a decline in attendance, and vice versa, even though the two, as noted above, are correlated and remain associated each with the other to about the same degree over time. The statements in this paragraph are based on a detailed analysis, numerical results of which are not presented here. The main point to be made is that we find a declining trend in both attendance and interest; and the evidence for each trend does not merely duplicate the evidence for the other, although it may well be that both trends are merely reflections of some general reorientation to organized religion that we have not measured directly.

In addition to the information on the recent change in respondent's interest in religion, we have measures of intergenerational change, obtained by asking the respondent whether his father and mother were more or less religious than the respondent (see Table 22). In both 1958 and 1971, over half the respondents indicated that their mothers were more religious than they, but only about one-

Table 22. Intergenerational Change in Religiosity

When your (father/mother) was about your age, was (he/she) more religious than you are, about as religious, or would you say (he/she) was less religious than you are?	*Percent Distribution*	
	1958	*1971*
Father		
More religious	32	33
About as religious	48	38
Less religious	21	29
	100	100
Mother		
More religious	54	58
About as religious	38	33
Less religious	8	10
	100	100

third of the fathers were more religious. The 1958 and 1971 distributions for mothers are rather similar, although there is a significant decrease in the proportion saying the mother was about as religious as the respondent, compensated by increases in both the proportions whose mothers were more religious and less religious. The 1958 and 1971 distributions for fathers show a greater difference, in particular a significant increase in the proportion saying their father was less religious. It would take a rather complicated and circumstantial interpretation of past changes in religiosity to account for these differences, assuming the reliability of the respondents' reports on their parents, about which we are perhaps entitled to be a little skeptical. On the surface, these data would seem to lend credence to the notion of cyclical variation in strength of religious interests. But one would do well not to press this hypothesis in the absence of both more detailed analysis of these data and better evidence of the historical variation in strength of interest in matters religious.

Two other indicators may be mentioned briefly. In 1958 and 1971, parents were asked, "In your family, do you ever say a prayer before meals?" The answer was affirmative for 72 percent of respondents in 1958 and 71 percent in 1971, not a significant difference. Results of a question on participation in church activities other than religious services are shown in Table 23. If we exclude

Table 23. Participation in Church Activities

Do you take part in any of the activities or organizations of your church (synagogue, temple) other than attending services? How often have you done these things, all told, during the last year? (excludes persons never attending services)	Percent Distribution	
	1958	*1971*
Yes		
Once a week or more	12	11
Less often	16	25
No	72	64
	100	100

respondents who never attend services, there is a statistically significant increase between 1958 and 1971 in this form of participation, as the proportion replying affirmatively rises from 28 percent to 36 percent. It may be noted that this evidence is contrary to that given earlier as to the decline in membership in church-connected organizations. The two questions are, of course, not the same; nevertheless, the discrepancy warns us against over-generalized statements about trends in religious activity and interest.

Communal Involvement

According to Lenski, whose 1958 survey provides the base line for many of our measures of religious change, communal involvement refers to the degree to which an individual's primary relations are limited to members of his own religious group.[1] In Table 24 we have three indicators of communal involvement, two of which take a normative form: is it wiser to marry within one's group; is it wiser to choose one's friends within the group? The third is behavioral: what proportion of one's friends actually are members of the same religious category?

A general summary applies to all three indicators and each of the three categories, Protestant, Catholic, and Jew. The extent of communal involvement diminished in the thirteen years between 1958 and 1971. Or, to phrase the finding differently, the dependence on religion as a basis for decisions about interpersonal relationships decreased. There are, however, some qualifications and elaborations of this summary.

In regard to intermarriage, although the proportion of Jews endorsing marriage only within the group decreased, as occurred for Protestants and Catholics, our samples of Jewish respondents are so small that we cannot rule out sampling fluctuations as the source of the ostensible change. For the two larger groups, however, the changes are clearly significant. Moreover, the more rapid change for Catholics than' for Protestants, resulting in a convergence of the two groups on this issue, is likewise statistically reliable.

As to the wisdom of choosing friends within the group, although the comparison shows a decrease for all three groups, only for Catholics is the change statistically significant. Again, the more rapid change for Catholics produces a significant convergence toward the Protestant fig-

[1] Gerhard Lenski, *The Religious Factor*, New York: Doubleday, 1961.

Table 24. Communal Involvement

As a general rule, do you think it is wiser for (Protestants/Catholics/Jewish people) to marry other (Protestant/Catholic/Jewish people) or not? (percent in each group saying "wiser")	1958	1971
Protestants	66	53
Catholics	80	59
Jews	92	76

As a general rule, do you think it is wiser for (Protestants/Catholics/Jewish people) to choose other (Protestant/Catholic/Jewish people) as their really close friends, or not? (percent in each group saying "wiser")		
Protestants	19	16
Catholics	30	9
Jews	38	24

Thinking of *your* closest friends, what proportion are (Protestants/Catholics/Jewish)? (percent in each group saying "all of them" or "nearly all of them")		
Protestants	45	30
Catholics	43	22
Jews	77	53

ure. Indeed, by 1971, Catholics supported the wisdom of in-group friendship choice even less strongly than Protestants.

For all three groups, the proportions actually having friends largely drawn from the same religious category decreased between 1958 and 1971. These changes were all significant, as is the greater rapidity of the Catholic change, resulting in a distinctly lower proportion of Catholics with almost exclusively Catholic friends than of Protestants choosing most of their friends among Protestants.

The decrease in communal involvement, particularly pronounced for Catholics, may have several causes. It may be related, for example, to the declining strength of religious beliefs; for if people are no longer so single-minded about their faith they may be less inclined to let doctrinal differences affect their secular associations. As we shall see (in the data on religious beliefs, shown later), respondents in 1971 more frequently asserted their right to question the teachings of their church than was true earlier. When Catholics were asked in 1958, "Do you believe that the Catholic Church is the only true Church established by God Himself, and that other churches were only established by men?," 66 percent of them responded affirmatively. In 1971 the figure was only 42 percent.

It appears that one possible source of decline in communal involvement can tentatively be ruled out. Since persons often form friendships and find their mates at school, if many Catholics attend parochial schools the opportunities for both Protestants and Catholics to be involved across communal lines would be diminished. But the evidence indicates no decrease in parochial school attendance. In 1954, Catholics were asked, "In grade or high school did you ever attend a parochial school?" In 1958 and 1971, they were asked, "Did you get any of your education in parochial schools or schools run by your church?" The percentage responding affirmatively was 58 in 1954, 63 in 1958, and 65 in 1971. The change from 1958 to 1971 is not significant. The significant change between 1954 and 1971 may well be due to the difference in wording, since the 1971 question was a little less specific. In any event, the ostensible change was in the direction of an increase in parochial school attendance, so that this change can hardly account for the decreasing communal involvement as measured by marriage and friendship norms. On the other hand, decreasing church attendance and decreasing participation in church-connected groups, may well be a factor reducing the exposure to potential friends or spouses of one's own faith.

The other side of the coin of communal involvement is a negative attitude toward out-groups. While the two need not go together, a strong preference for social relationships within one's own religious community may be converted into a stereotypic or hostile view of the other communities. The evidence on decreasing communal involvement suggests that we may find some reduction in negative attitudes of this kind. Indeed, it is clear that the two major Christian categories are alike in that their adherents now express less unfavorable images of Jews than was true a decade or so earlier. In Table 25 we see that for both Protestants and Catholics the proportion imputing unfairness to Jews in business dealings has decreased. The decrease would appear to have been more rapid for Catholics, although the contrast in rates of change is only on the borderline of statistical significance. The higher incidence of negative attitudes on this question among Protestants is, however, statistically reliable. On the question of whether the Jewish people have been trying to get too much power in the United States, Protestants and Catholics alike have decreased in willingness to endorse the affirmative.

Table 25. Attitudes Toward Jews

Compared with (Protestants/Catholics), do you think that the Jewish people as a whole are more fair, as fair, or less fair in their *business dealings*? (percent of each group saying Jewish less fair)	1958	1971
Protestants	47	37
Catholics	46	27
Do you feel that the Jewish people have been trying to get *too much power* in the country, or not? (percent of each group saying "yes")		
Protestants	27	22
Catholics	26	20

A similar question was put to Protestants only: Do you feel that Catholics have been trying to get too much power in this country, or not?" In both 1958 and 1971, just 25 percent of the Protestants answered "Yes." We recall that the election of the first Catholic President, in 1960, came between the two surveys, while the issue of governmental aid to parochial education has been prominent from time to time in recent years. No doubt some balancing out of contrary tendencies resulted in the stability of this particular statistic.

Religious Beliefs

In addition to estimates of change in religious beliefs, we shall provide some evidence on ambiguities that are inherent in the attempt to measure such beliefs. Given this evidence, the skeptic may wonder whether the estimates of change are to be given any credence at all. But some of the changes are too large to be explained easily on grounds of errors of measurement.

We begin with a question on belief in God (Table 26). Here the change, if any, concerns a very small fraction of the population, and we must resort to showing a decimal value for the percentages so that it will not be lost in rounding error. The wording of the question appears to be of some consequence. When it is explicitly communicated to the respondent that to be "uncertain" is an acceptable answer, there is a significant increase in the proportion falling in that category, or so we infer from the comparison of the 1958 and 1959 distributions. Whether there is a genuine increase in uncertainty of belief over time remains unclear from this question, although we provide further evidence on that issue later. Between the 1958 and 1971 surveys, which used the same wording of the question on belief in God, there was a small, but not statistically significant increase in proportion uncertain. On the other hand, with the uncertain respondents removed from the two distributions, the decrease in percentage affirming belief in God was clearly significant, despite its small size.

The question on belief in life after death shows an even stronger effect of wording, perhaps induced by the preamble to the question used in 1959. The explicit provision of an uncertain category seemingly causes that category to gain respondents at the expense of both the numbers affirming and denying life after death (compare the 1958 and 1959 distributions in Table 26). The comparison between 1958 and 1971, however, is not confounded by a wording variation, and we find that the proportion uncertain remains about constant, while the proportion answer-

Table 26. Religious Beliefs

Some people wonder whether [or not]ª there is a God. How do you feel—do you believe there is a God, or not [or are you uncertain]ª?	Percent Distribution		
	1958	1959	1971
Yes	96.6	93.2	94.0
Uncertain	2.3	5.2	3.5
No	1.1	1.6	2.5
	100.0	100.0	100.0

Do you believe in life after death, or not? [1958, 1971]
Some people think there is a life after death; others don't think there is, and still others feel uncertain. In your opinion, is there a life after death or not, or are you uncertain? [1959]

Yes	74	66	65
Uncertain	12	27	13
No [excludes those who do not believe in God]	14	7	22
	100	100	100

Do you feel you have the right to question what your church teaches, or not?

Yes	68	. . .	81
Unsure	4	. . .	2
No	28	. . .	17
	100		100

Do you believe that someone who doesn't believe in God can be a good American, or not?

Can	57	. . .	77
Unsure	7	. . .	4
Cannot	36	. . .	19
	100		100

When you have decisions to make in your everyday life, do you ask yourself what God would want you to do?

Often	35	. . .	38
Sometimes	46	. . .	41
Never	19	. . .	21
	100		100

ª Words included only in 1959.

ing "no" gains some 8 percentage points at the expense of the proportion "yes." It is curious that the 1959 percentage "yes," given the apparent defections to the uncertain category, is about the same as the 1971 percentage "yes," where such defections are not in evidence, whereas the proportion definitely answering "no" is significantly greater in 1971 than in the 1959 distribution. It appears that we must conclude that a growing fraction of the population does not believe in life after death. This conclusion, it should be noted, holds independently of the change in belief in God, since persons not believing in God were excluded from the analysis of change in belief in life after death.

Disregarding the content of beliefs, people are insisting more strongly on their right to make up their own minds about religious doctrines. In 1958, about two-thirds of the respondents averred that they have the right to question what their church teaches; in 1971, about four-fifths asserted this right (see third question in Table 26).

Although an overwhelming majority of respondents affirm their own belief in God, most of them are somewhat tolerant of disbelief on the part of others. Such tolerance increased measurably between 1958 and 1971, as the percentage agreeing that one who does not believe in God can be a good American rose from 57 to 77 (see fourth question in Table 26).

Whereas all four of the questions discussed thus far suggest an erosion of religious belief in one sense or another, the final question in Table 26 shows no significant change in the proportion of respondents who indicate that they govern decisions in everyday life by what they think God would want them to do. Again we are warned that the apparent erosion in religious beliefs, suggested by the other four questions in this table, may be a one-sided description of trends. People may well retain their habits of personal piety while coming to feel less constrained to endorse conventional or official doctrines.

Further evidence on certainty of belief appears in Table 27. As we noted, the 1959 survey worded the initial question on belief in God in such a way as to suggest that

Table 27. Certainty of Belief in God

Many people, including saints and great religious leaders, have had doubts from time to time throughout their lives about the existence of God. Which of these statements about your belief in God's existence best fits the way you feel?	Percent Distribution[a]	
	1959	1971
Not sure. I just don't know	2	6
Not too sure. My ideas are probably correct, but I really don't know.	7	15
Rather sure. Many of the facts I know support my belief.	23	31
Very sure. At present I have no doubt that my beliefs are right.	68	48
	100	100

[a] Based on those answering, "Yes [there is a God]."

"uncertain" was an acceptable answer. Moreover, those giving a definite "yes" answer were further asked how sure they were of their beliefs. In 1959, two-thirds selected the answer, very sure; in the 1971 survey, just under one-half chose this alternative, while increased proportions selected each of the other alternatives, expressing various degrees of doubt about one's own beliefs. The wording of the question contains a point that should be kept in mind in interpreting these results—that doubts about one's beliefs are not the same as disbelief.

Values

As is true of the other topics presented in this study, we do not have a comprehensive or well-structured set of measurements on changes in the values people affirm. Our opportunistic selection of questions from earlier studies has, however, resulted in some interesting, if fragmentary, evidence of shifts in what people hold to be moral and desirable.

From Table 28 we learn that there is an increased moral tolerance for gambling in the population now, as compared with 1958. The matter remains an issue that divides the citizenry, however, with a strong one-fourth of the respondents in 1971 (as compared with one-third in 1958) still maintaining that gambling is always wrong.

The shift in the moral stand on divorce has been more dramatic. Between the two surveys the proportion stating that divorce is sometimes wrong—therefore, presumably, sometimes right—increased from 48 to 70 percent; and there was even a small increase in the fraction holding that it is never wrong.

On the morality of obeying the law, we have the hypothetical question, "If you were driving in another state and got a ticket for parking just a few minutes overtime while getting your lunch, would you bother to pay the fine?" In 1958, 82 percent said they would pay the fine; in 1971, the figure was 84 percent, not significantly different. For those giving this answer, the matter was pursued with another question, "Would you pay it even if you were in a big hurry and knew that the police in that town would never bother you if you didn't pay the fine?" Some 77 percent of those answering yes on the preceding question gave the same answer to this version in 1958; in 1971, the figure was almost the same, 78 percent (the difference is not significant). One's own views of the ethics of paying traffic fines will no doubt color his interpretation of these results, which indicate, after all, that about one-third of the population will not pay if they think they can get away

Table 28. Moral Issues

How do you feel about gambling? From the moral standpoint, would you say it is	Percent Distribution	
	1958	1971
Always wrong	32	25
Usually wrong	13	9
Sometimes wrong	47	49
Never wrong	8	17
	100	100
From the moral standpoint, how do you feel about divorce?		
Always wrong	23	8
Usually wrong	20	10
Sometimes wrong	48	70
Never wrong	9	12
	100	100

without paying. But if such an answer does connote disrespect for law, it is at least noteworthy that these results suggest no increase in disrespect.

One of the questions in the values domain for which we have evidence on change is particularly interesting to sociologists because of its association with the controversial Protestant Ethic thesis. We shall not review that thesis as it was presented in Lenski's report on the 1958 study (cited earlier), but merely note that aspects of his work were partially replicated in the 1966 DAS survey, and his hypothesis has been reconsidered in other publications.[1] Here we shall be content to describe changes in the pattern of responses to the particular question that Lenski devised to get at value orientations regarding work:

Would you please look at this card and tell me which thing on this list you would most prefer in a job [mar-

[1] Howard Schuman, "The Religious Factor in Detroit: Review, Replication, and Reanalysis," *American Sociological Review*, 36 (1971): 30–48; Otis Dudley Duncan and David L. Featherman, "Psychological and Cultural Factors in the Process of Occupational Achievement," *Social Science Research*, 1 (1972): 121–145.

ried women were asked: which thing you would want most for your husband's job]?

[A] High income
[B] No danger of being fired
[C] Working hours are short, lots of free time
[D] Chances for advancement
[E] The work is important and gives a feeling of accomplishment.

Which comes next? Which is third most important?
Which is fourth most important [in 1958: Which is least important]?

This sequence of questions has the effect of requesting the respondent to place the five work values in order of their preference ranking for himself. Some respondents failed to complete all the questions and a few tied ranks or gave inconsistent answers. It seems best to eliminate these from the present analysis. We may then compute the average rank assigned to each value; the averages are shown in Figure 5.

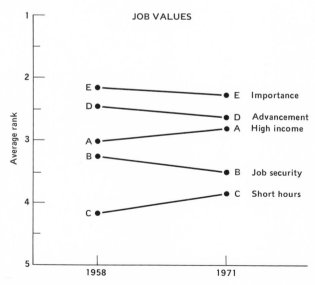

Figure 5. Average Ranks of Five Values in a Job

Although the values have the same rank order in 1971 as they did in 1958, there are unmistakable shifts in their relative popularity. High income and short hours ranked appreciably higher in 1971 than in 1958, the greatest gain being recorded by the latter. Correlatively, importance of the work, chance for advancement, and job security declined in popularity relative to income and short hours, although they retained the same positions with respect to each other. In terms of the interpretation that Lenski gave to these values, we should have to conclude that there was some attenuation of the Protestant Ethic in the Detroit population over the thirteen-year period. It is true, however, that the values most clearly expressive of that orientation continue to be ranked high most often.

One wonders how much the ranking of these values may reflect relatively short-term situational factors, as distinct from long-run drifts in value orientations. For example, the decline of concern for job security, relative to income and hours, may reflect the fact that more respondents are tending to take job security for granted. Thus, the question, which we are interpreting as a reflection of values in work, may also reflect which facets of a job are seen as most problematic at a given point in time. Having granted this qualification, it does seem inescapable that the instrumental, or even hedonistic, values suggested by high income and short working hours, are gaining at the expense of the values intrinsic to the work, most notably the idea that doing the job in itself gives one a sense of accomplishment.

The last "values" question to be considered may seem to be inappropriately characterized as such. It is the question on social class identification displayed in Table 29. Answers to this question have sometimes been taken to represent respondents' estimates of where they stand in a hierarchy of social stratification, or how they see their economic interests in terms of alignments with other groups in the society. There is growing evidence, however, that the question taps, if it does not directly measure, a variety of value orientations. To some extent, as Duncan and

Table 29. Subjective Social Class Identification

A large community like the Detroit area is made up of many kinds of groups. If you had to place yourself in one of these groups, would you say that you are in the:	Percent Distribution				
	Upper class	Middle class	Working class	Lower class	Total
1956	2	35	61	1	100
1958 (2 alternatives)	...	32	68	...	100
1971	2	46	48	4	100
1957 (Wayne County)	2	32	64	2	100
1971 (Wayne County)	2	38	54	6	100
1953 (Mothers; wording varied)	2	42	54	2	100
1971 (Mothers)	1	47	46	6	100

Featherman argue, it seems to work like a projective question; that is, the respondent interprets the question in terms of what is salient to him about status in the society, and not necessarily in terms of what is salient to the sociologist. Obviously, it will take a good deal of analysis to determine just what social distinctions and ideological positions respondents are trying to convey when they answer this question. We have evidence, for example, that women interpret it somewhat differently from men. But this is not the place to pursue such questions; even an elaborate analysis will probably yield only tantalizingly suggestive answers. We simply record here the result that since the 1950s there has been a significant increase in the proportion of respondents self-identified as middle class. To some extent, this may be a function of the rising level of real income in the Detroit population, the upgrading of educational levels, and other gains in socioeconomic status. But we wish to leave open the possibility that this change may have other dimensions as well. The apparent increase in proportion responding lower class, like the sex difference, is an indication that there may be a somewhat complicated set of processes lying behind the general shift toward the middle class category.

Political Participation

Our only direct question on the citizen's actual involvement in the political process, as distinct from his opinions and attitudes about such involvement, is the following: "Have you ever helped campaign for a party or candidate during an election—like putting in time or contributing money?" One-sixth (16 percent) of the respondents answered affirmatively in 1954; by 1971, the fraction had risen to one-third (33 percent). In view of the large supply of official data on voting, supplemented by repeated national surveys of the American electorate, we did not investigate election turnout or other such indicators of political interest. Perhaps this is just as well, since a judicious review of these materials has disclosed the severe difficulties in securing unambiguous interpretations of the changes revealed by election returns.[1]

One consequence of a change in political involvement, if it is not wholly superficial, should be an alteration in the amount of information that citizens have about government and politics. In his analysis of the 1957 survey, Eldersveld found that respondents with "high exposure" to the political parties were much more likely to know the names of their congressmen and senators, and somewhat more likely to know the terms of their offices, than those with "no exposure."[2] Given the increase in campaign involvement noted above, we were curious to learn whether there would be any improvement between 1957 and 1971 in the level of political information, as this might be revealed by the little "test" that was included in the baseline survey taken in the earlier year. The test consisted of asking the respondent to name the United States senators from Michigan and the congressman from his own district,

[1] Philip E. Converse, "Change in the American Electorate," in Angus Campbell and Philip E. Converse (eds.), *The Human Meaning of Social Change,* New York: Russell Sage Foundation, 1972.

[2] Samuel J. Eldersveld, *Political Parties: A Behavioral Analysis,* Chicago: Rand McNally, 1964, pp. 493–494.

and to state how long the term of office is for a senator and for a congressman. The data in Table 30 for both 1957 and 1971 are limited to respondents in Wayne County.

It appears that we must be cautious in making any generalization about a shift in level of political information. There was indeed a substantial increase, more than 20 percentage points, in the proportion able to name at least one senator. There was also a distinct improvement in the proportion knowing the name of their congressman. However, there was no change in the fraction stating correctly the length of a senator's term, and actually quite a decrease in the proportion answering correctly as to the term of a congressman. We can, of course, resort to averaging these disparate changes. For example, if we allow one point for a correct answer to each question (one-half point if only one senator is named), the average score works out at 1.03 in 1957 and 1.18 in 1971, or 26 percent of the possible perfect score of four points in 1957, as against 29 percent in 1971. Clearly, the bulk of the population "flunked" the test in both years, and the improvement between years was very minor, at best.

We can only speculate about the reasons for this mixed performance. It should be noted that the four test items do appear to be related, since a correct answer on one item is positively associated with a correct answer on each other item. This holds true in both years; moreover, there was no significant change in the pattern or degree of inter-

Table 30. Political Information Test

	Percent Giving Correct Answer	
	1957	1971
Do you happen to know the names of the United States senators from Michigan? (percent naming at least one correctly)	35	56
Can you tell me how long the term of office is for a United States senator?	18	17
Do you know who the Congressman from this district is?	20	29
Can you tell me how long the term of office is for a Congressman?	41	27

item association. On this evidence, one might hold that the four questions are more or less interchangeable indicators of the same general trait—level of political information. The contrary patterns of change are, however, a little hard to account for on this theory. What is striking here is that there is improvement in ability to name the officeholders, but deterioration in ability to state the length of their terms of office. We have no easy way to take account of the possibility that the officeholders in 1971 were better known, simply for various idiosyncratic reasons, than their counterparts in 1957.

One possible clue to an explanation for the contrary shifts is suggested by Table 31. Here we find that there has been a very pronounced change in the source of political news, a change that is readily summarized in the statement that people relied much more heavily on television in 1971 than they did in 1954, when newspapers were still the primary source. Television gained at the expense of radio as well, while the importance of radio relative to newspapers did not change. Our speculation is that television may do a much better job of keeping the citizen reminded of who the officeholders are than it does in educating the public in elementary civics.

We might note that the 1957 survey was conducted some three to five months after the 1956 presidential election, while the 1971 survey was in the field approximately five to ten months after the 1970 election, in which there was no contest for president. Another contextual factor

Table 31. Sources of Political News

Of all the ways of getting the news about government officials and bureaus, which would you say you depend on the most?	*Percent Distribution*	
	1954	*1971*
Newspapers	57	40
Radio	13	10
Television	19	40
(other and not ascertained)	11	10
	100	100

which we could not control is that the 1957 survey was almost exclusively devoted to questions about political attitudes and behavior; the information test was preceded by more than sixty questions on these topics. In 1971, much less of the questionnaire was devoted to this kind of material. On both counts—the timing of the election and the context of the remainder of the interview—it seems plausible that the respondents in 1957 might have had a slight advantage. We tend to doubt, however, that such contextual factors are of major significance in the purely cognitive performance called for by the information test.

To return to our earlier notion, the increase in political participation, if it had any causal influence on political information, evidently had a very selective effect on knowledge of officeholders, but not on knowledge of the constitutional framework of politics. The differential change in these two kinds of information is one of many tantalizing findings for which we have no convincing interpretation, although in a rough sense it is consistent with Eldersveld's finding that political exposure increases recognition of the officeholders more than it does knowledge of the terms of office.

Public Affairs

Whereas the material on political participation looks at the citizen in an active role—taking part in elections or informing himself about politics—the data in this section treat him as a passive consumer of the outputs of public institutions or evaluator of their performance. With the well-advertised rise of "consumerism" in recent years, we shall not be surprised if the public seems more critical of the services it receives than it was in the past.

In Table 32 we show the distribution of "good," "fair," and "poor" scores awarded by respondents to the performance of seven kinds of institutions in 1959 and 1971. One uniform result stands out: each of these institutions is seen as doing a good job by fewer respondents in 1971 than in 1959. In every case, there is a significant shift out of the good category and into the fair; in all cases but two—radio and television networks, and scientists—there is also a significant gain for the poor category. This monotonously repeated pattern suggests that something more than the actual performance of the seven institutions may be at stake. It is, to be sure, logically possible that all seven are actually performing less effectively in 1971 than they did a dozen years earlier. But a simpler explanation would be that the public has escalated its standards across the board; that is, it has simply adopted more demanding criteria for all organizations rendering service to the public.

We do not imply, however, that the only change has been that of taking a dimmer view of every agency. To the contrary, is the fact that the changes, although all in the same direction, are at quite different rates. The Boy Scouts and scientists, evaluated quite favorably in 1959 by comparison with the other institutions, lost only a little ground and retained their relatively favored positions. But note the contrast between the doctors and the colleges: they were in about the same reasonably high position in 1959, with three-fourths of their ratings good. By 1971, the doctors had declined appreciably to three-fifths good ratings, but

81

Table 32. Evaluation of Institutions

Now here is a list of organizations and groups that people have different opinions about. After each one, would you tell me if, in your opinion, it is doing a good job, just a fair job, or a poor job.		Percent Distribution			
		Good	Fair	Poor	Total
How about the radio and TV networks?	1959	55	37	8	100
	1971	46	44	10	100
most high schools in this country?	1959	45	45	10	100
	1971	29	46	25	100
most doctors?	1959	76	20	4	100
	1971	62	30	8	100
most colleges?	1959	75	22	3	100
	1971	42	44	14	100
most scientists?	1959	83	15	2	100
	1971	78	19	3	100
the Federal Courts?	1959	63	30	7	100
	1971	24	46	30	100
the Boy Scouts?	1959	93	6	1	100
	1971	87	10	3	100
most Michigan State officials?	1971	22	53	25	100

colleges had declined precipitously to two-fifths. The Federal Courts in 1959 were seen in a more favorable light than the radio and television networks or the high schools; but in 1971 they received the lowest rating among the seven institutions. The high schools, too, slipped rather badly, though not so seriously as the courts, while the networks lost comparatively little ground.

We are thus led to a second obvious generalization: the institutions suffering the greatest loss in their ratings are the three—the schools, the colleges, and the courts— that have been centers of controversy in recent years. If a causal inference is justified here, then we are warned that the 1959–1971 changes may not necessarily be prognostic of future trends. Other institutions may become the foci of public discontent, and the ones losing public confidence in the 1960s could perhaps regain some of it in future years.

The last group listed in Table 32, most Michigan State officials, was rated in this particular format only in 1971. A fairly similar question appears in Table 33, along with a parallel one on local government. If we add "good" and "very good" together in Table 33 for the 1971 distribution of ratings of state government, we get a distribution roughly the same as the one at the bottom of Table 32. It seems reasonable, therefore, to assume that the change in ratings of state government from 1954 to 1971 shown in Table 33 is representative of what we would have found had there been a base-line measurement for Table 32. We conjecture that the decline in performance rating for state government would be very much like that measured for Federal Courts, were the two on the same scale of measurement and for the same years. That is, the loss in confidence in state officials has been one of the more decided losses of this kind. In any event, using Table 33 alone we can say for sure that the deterioration of performance rating has been more pronounced for the state government than for local government. In 1954, state officials and agencies had somewhat more favorable ratings than did the local ones, whereas the comparison had been reversed by 1971.

Still another series of ratings is offered in Figure 6, here in terms of satisfaction with three major local governmental services. Respondents in 1971 were rather less sat-

Table 33. Evaluation of State and Local Government

Do you think the [name of local community] officials and bureaus are doing a poor, fair, good, or very good job?	*Percent Distribution*				
	Poor	*Fair*	*Good*	*V.G.*	*Total*
1954	6	40	42	12	100
1971	18	48	29	5	100

And the state government—do you think the state officials and bureaus are doing a poor, fair, good, or very good job?

1954	4	33	52	11	100
1971	19	56	23	2	100

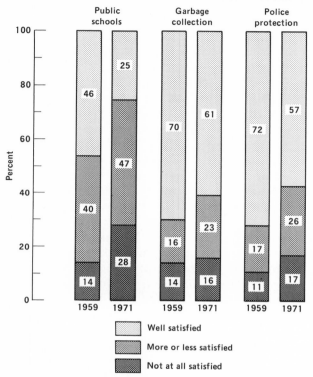

Figure 6. Evaluation of Government Services (Percent Distribution).

In general, would you say that you are well satisfied, more or less satisfied, or not at all satisfied with the job the public schools here are doing? . . . with the city garbage collection here? . . . with the protection provided for your neighborhood by the police?

isfied than those interviewed in 1959 with the public schools, garbage collection, and police services. Again, we might assume an overall decrease in willingness to express satisfaction with anything, but that would not explain the fact that the schools lost ground rapidly while the drop in ratings of garbage collection was fairly modest.

Instead of asking respondents how well groups and agencies perform, we might have asked them about their confidence in future performance. The one item of this general type relates to science: "Given enough time and money, almost all of man's important problems can be solved by science." (Respondents were asked to choose among strongly agree, agree, disagree, and strongly disagree.) In 1959, 43 percent said agree or strongly agree; by 1971, this had declined to 32 percent. Since about three-fifths of respondents think that scientists are doing a good job, it must be that many respondents realize that "a good job" may not be good enough to solve all our problems. In other words, it seems entirely possible that what we are measuring in these several series of evaluations is partly an increasing sophistication about the difficulties faced by public institutions.

We do not have questions that require the respondent explicitly to take into account the problems that government and other public institutions are attempting to solve, as well as their performance in solving them. Tangentially relevant is the question presented in Table 34, which asks respondents to weigh the costs and benefits of government services in general. In 1954, just over half the population felt that costs and benefits were about equal, and only a third felt that government asks more from the public than it returns in help and services. By 1971, the two proportions had just reversed; now, the most frequent answer is that costs outweigh benefits.

Table 34. Costs and Benefits of Government

Which one of these statements comes closest to your own opinion	*Percent Distribution*	
	1954	*1971*
The help and services that the public gets from the government is worth what it asks from the public.	53	29
The government asks more from the public than it gives in help and services.	32	53
The public gets more from the government than it gives the government.	15	18
	100	100

One other means of gaining some insight into the deterioration of performance ratings is to look at public agencies, not from the standpoint of the services they render, but in terms of their desirability as employers. For if local governmental agencies, for example, were seen as doing a worse job primarily because of internal deficiencies which are not shared with private firms, then we might expect their image as employers to deteriorate. In studying the prestige of public employment, we are dealing with a replication of a replication. In the 1954 DAS, Janowitz and Wright sought to measure the trend by duplicating some of the questions which had been used by L. D. White in his Chicago study of 1929. Their comparisons with White's data suggested that there had been a marked improvement in the prestige of jobs in government agencies relative to similar jobs with private employers over the preceding quarter of a century. The conclusion was subject to some uncertainty, owing to the shift in study locale from Chicago to Detroit and the differences in sampling and survey techniques.[1]

We tried to repeat the procedure of Janowitz and Wright exactly, so that any difference between the 1954 and 1971 results would be due solely to changing assessments of prestige and not to variations in technique. There remains some question as to whether we were entirely successful. The most obvious trend in Table 35 is that for each of the four illustrative occupations, the percentage who declared there is "no difference" between the prestige of public and private employment diminished considerably over the seventeen-year period. Now, the alternative, "no difference" was not explicitly offered to the respondent, and his answer was coded in this category only if he declined to make a choice between the two alternatives presented to him. It may be that our interviewers in 1971 were more assiduous in probing for a decision than was true in 1954.

[1] Morris Janowitz and Deil Wright, "The Prestige of Public Employment: 1929 and 1954," *Public Administration Review*, 16 (Winter 1956): 15–21.

Table 35. Prestige of Public Employment

We'd like to know what people think of government jobs and government workers. If these jobs are about the same in kind of work, pay, and so forth, which has the most prestige?		*Private*	*Public*	*No dif-ference*	*Total*
			Percent Distribution		
Stenographer in a life insurance company	1954	27	53	20	100
. . . in the city tax assessor's office	1971	33	59	8	100
Accountant in a private accounting firm	1954	42	42	16	100
. . . in the Detroit Dept. of Pub. Works	1971	55	40	5	100
Night watchman in a bank	1954	43	37	20	100
. . . in the city hall	1971	45	46	9	100
Doctor on staff of private hospital	1954	58	27	15	100
. . . in the Detroit Receiving Hospital	1971	61	33	6	100

Let us, therefore, eliminate the "no difference" category and recompute the percentages of respondents attributing the higher prestige to the job with a public employer. In regard to the occupation of stenographer, the preference for public employers declined from 66 to 64 percent; and for accountants it declined from 50 to 42 percent. Only the latter difference is large enough to rule out sampling fluctuations as the explanation. For the night watchman, the prestige of public employment increased by virtue of the shift from 46 to 51 percent favoring that alternative, and for doctors, there was also an upward shift, from 32 to 35 percent. Neither of these changes, however, is large enough to be statistically significant in the sense of ruling out chance variation as the source of the apparent change.

Our finding, then, is that the evidence is mixed. The only change we can assert with confidence pertains to a single occupation, accountant. It should be noted that the ostensible deterioration in the prestige of public employment for this occupation could be due to a worsening of the image of the Detroit Department of Public Works, in particular, rather than a drop in the attractiveness of the public sector in general. We do not, of course, have any definite evidence to this effect. Perhaps the safest conclusion to draw is that the pronounced trend of improvement in the prestige of public employment discerned by Janowitz and Wright in 1954 had about peaked out by that time, so that subsequent changes may largely reflect idiosyncratic features of particular occupations or particular public agencies. In any case, we do not find the decisive deterioration in prestige of public employment that we might have expected from the drastic decline in favorable performance ratings of public agencies.

Political Orientations

In this study, we did not try to measure trends in political partisanship, changes in the distribution of "liberal" and "conservative" ideologies, and reactions to transitory political issues, since these matters are dealt with by the public opinion polls and well-known studies of electoral behavior. We did, however, choose a few questions to elicit respondents' views of how the polity should be run. Some of the issues broached are clearly related to classical controversies in political philosophy which have been before the country since its founding and give every promise of being perennial. For example, it is gratifying that we can respond directly, if in a modest way, to a need expressed in a pioneer project in social reporting:

> Perhaps the most obvious function that we expect our institutions to perform is that of protecting our individual freedom. . . . Freedom can be abridged not only by government action, but also by the social and economic ostracism and discrimination that results from popular intolerance. There is accordingly a need for survey data that can discern any major changes in the degree of tolerance and in the willingness to state unpopular points of view. . . .[1]

Our measure of "popular tolerance" is obtained from a question exploring the limits of free speech, as interpreted by the respondent (Table 36). There was clearly a greater willingness to interpret free speech liberally in 1971 than in 1958. Although fewer than half the respondents, even in the later year, are willing to extend the concept to encompass toleration of the advocacy of Communism and Fascism, the proportion defining free speech this broadly showed a substantial increase for both these items. The same was true in regard to permitting speeches against religion: less than half were willing to do so in 1959, as

[1] U.S. Department of Health, Education, and Welfare, *Toward a Social Report*, Washington: U.S. Government Printing Office, 1969, p. xxi.

Table 36. Opinions on Freedom of Speech

In our country the Constitution guarantees the right of free speech to everyone. In your opinion, does this include the right for someone to make speeches	Percent Saying "Yes"	
	1958	1971
criticizing what the President does?	72	75
against religion?	47	59
in favor of Fascism or dictatorship?	37	48
in favor of Communism?	35	44

against nearly three-fifths in 1971. Only in regard to speeches criticizing the President was there too small a shift in the liberal direction to register as statistically significant; but affirmative responses to this item remained at the comparatively high level of three-quarters of the population.

A decline in "popular intolerance"—although some might prefer to interpret it as a decline in patriotism—is likewise suggested by the reactions to this proposition: "Every American family should be required by law to own a flag." In 1958, 38 percent of the respondents agreed, but in 1971, only 17 percent did so.

In regard to the respondent's own sense of his freedom to state an unpopular view, should he hold one, we do not have a really adequate measure, but the question dealt with in Table 37 is suggestive. First, we may note that the substantive issue of intervention in the affairs of another country is one on which there has been a major shift of opinion. We see in the table that almost half the respondents in 1971 thought the United States should not interfere in a South American revolution, whereas only a quarter of those responding in 1956 took this view. Nearly a half were in favor of intervention to the extent of sending arms to fight the Communist revolutionaries in 1956, but only a third in 1971. When asked whether "most people in Detroit" would agree with the position taken by the respondent, the affirmative answer was forthcoming in 86 percent of the cases in 1956, but in only 68 percent in 1971. Thus, in the later year, it would seem that more people were under the impression that they were stating a minority view.

Table 37. Opinions on Intervention

If a revolution takes place in a country in South America and it looks as though the Communist side might win, what action should we take?	Percent Distribution		
		1971	
	1956	Respond- ents	"Most People"[a]
Do not interfere	26	48	56
Send arms to the side fighting the Communists	47	33	29
Send U.S. troops in to fight the Communist group	27	19	15
	100	100	100

[a] Do you think that most people in the Detroit area would agree with you about this? What would they choose [asked in 1971 only]?

To that extent, we have evidence of increased willingness to express unpopular opinions. Interestingly enough, there actually was no "right" answer to the follow-up question in either year, if we interpret "most people" to mean more than half of the people, since no one of the three alternatives commanded a clear majority. But the division of actual opinion in 1956 and 1971 was much the same, so that a respondent who guessed that "most people" agree with him would be as close to being correct in one year as in the other. Yet, as we have seen, the perception that one belongs to a majority dropped substantially. Whether respondents interpret this perceived decrease in consensus as equivalent to greater freedom for themselves, in expressing opinions, or merely as greater confusion about what is the right thing to do, is not known.

From one point of view, willingness to tolerate expression of unpopular ideas is virtually synonymous with willingness to entertain proposals for social change. Most changes, one realizes in retrospect, begin with behavior that is deviant in the statistical sense of being uncommon, and often, also, in the sociological sense of being contrary to popularly endorsed norms. Having found an increasing tolerance for unpopular views, we need not be surprised by the discovery, which is conveyed by Table 38, that the

Table 38. Willingness to Change How Country Is Run

People feel differently about making changes in the way our country is run. Which of these four statements do you think is best?	Percent Distribution	
	1956	*1971*
We should rarely, if ever, make changes in the way our country is run.	2	2
We should be very cautious of making changes in the way our country is run.	49	42
We should feel free to make changes in the way our country is run.	37	32
We must constantly make changes in the way our country is run.	12	24
	100	100

proportion of people willing to see constant changes in the way our country is run rose from 12 to 24 percent between 1956 and 1971. Each of the other three alternative responses offered on the question of willingness to see changes made, lost proportionally to the most liberal alternative, so that their attractiveness, relative to each other, did not change. A change in the same direction is suggested by Table 39, where the question refers both to the Founding Fathers of this country and its Constitution in a way that one would expect to load it strongly against an expression of willingness to change. Yet, the proportion endorsing the need for frequent constitutional changes increased between 1956 and 1971 from 65 to 76 percent.

Another sacred symbol of the polity, the national anthem, was the subject of still another question on this general theme of willingness to change: "Many people find *The Star-Spangled Banner* difficult to sing. If a new and appropriate national anthem were written, would you *object* to substituting it for *The Star-Spangled Banner?*" In 1956, one-fourth (24 percent) of the respondents answered "No," that is, they would not object to the change; in 1971, the fraction had risen to about three in seven (45 percent).

One final question on the respondent's orientation to political philosophy is not related in an obvious way to the

Table 39. Willingness to Change Constitution

Which of these two statements do you agree with more?	Percent endorsing	
	1956	*1971*
The Founding Fathers had so much wisdom that our Constitution handles most modern problems very well.	35	24
While the Founding Fathers were very wise, the Constitution they wrote needs frequent changes to bring it up to date.	65	76
	100	100

issues of freedom of expression and willingness to change, but is ostensibly an indicator of "democratic" versus "elitist" leanings. The respondent was asked: "Which of these two kinds of men would make the best official for a town or city government? A man who is as much like the average person in the town as possible, so that he can understand and help the common man? A man who is superior to the average man in order to make wise decisions for the town?" In view of the linkage, vigorously espoused in recent years, between the necessity for basic changes in our sociopolitical structure and the desirability of achieving what is called a "participatory democracy," it is perhaps surprising that the elitist alternative in this question actually gained a few adherents: the proportion endorsing the "man who is superior to the average man" rose from 37 percent in 1956 to 42 percent in 1971, a clearly significant though only moderately large shift. Evidently, the increased willingness of the population to see changes in the polity does not necessarily connote an enhanced desire for democratization of the conduct of government, in the sense implied by the question.

The remainder of our material on political attitudes relates to the respondent's perception of the meaningfulness of his own role in the political process. Questions of this type are sometimes said to measure the respondent's sense of political efficacy. Whether this is a very stable or unitary dimension of one's outlook on politics and government may perhaps be questioned. In any event, as we learned, its measurement is tricky. In the 1971 survey, the six statements listed in Table 40 occurred in the sequence 6, 1, 2, 3, 4, 5 in Form A of the questionnaire, and in the reverse sequence, 5, 4, 3, 2, 1, 6 in Form B, identifying the statements with the numerals given in Table 40. (A statement

Table 40. Opinions on Politics and Government

		Percent Distribution				
		Strongly Agree	Agree	Dis-agree	Strongly Disagree	Total
1. So many other people	1954	3	7	42	48	100
vote in elections that	1971	2	10	56	32	100
it doesn't matter much	1957[a]		7		93	100
whether I vote or not	1971[a]		13		87	100
2. People like me don't	1954	2	19	53	26	100
have any say about	1971A	4	27	57	12	100
what the government	1971B	7	34	54	5	100
does	1957[a]		27		73	100
	1971A[a]		33		67	100
	1971B[a]		44		56	100
3. Sometimes politics	1954	8	59	26	7	100
and government seem	1971A	12	53	30	5	100
so complicated that a	1971B	17	56	24	3	100
person like me can't	1957[a]		62		38	100
really understand	1971A[a]		68		32	100
what is going on	1971B[a]		76		24	100
4. Voting is the only way	1954	12	53	31	4	100
that people like me	1971	12	48	35	5	100
can have any say						
about how the gov-						
ernment runs things						
5. I don't think public	1954	7	21	58	14	100
officials care much	1971A	6	42	49	3	100
about what people	1971B	10	40	45	5	100
like me think						
6. Public officials really	1957[a]		79		21	100
care about what	1971A[a]		43		57	100
people like me think	1971B[a]		50		50	100

[a] Respondents in Wayne County only.

about science, which we reported on earlier, followed statement 4 in Form A and statement 5 in Form B.) It will be noted that 5 and 6 are ostensibly the same statement, with the wording reversed. For some reason, on Form B the reversal does not affect the proportion agreeing; the split is 50–50 with either wording. On Form A, however, 52 percent disagree with statement 5, thereby expressing a positive sense of their political efficacy, whereas only 43 percent agree with statement 6, ostensibly an equivalent response. In Table 40, we have shown separate distributions for the two forms for each statement that produced a significant difference. It is perhaps suggestive that the two statements (1 and 4) that did not show response variation due to order of presentation are the two concerning the advisability of voting, despite the probability that one's single vote may count for little. We conjecture that the propositions about voting really have the sense of normative statements: one is taught to believe or is supposed to believe that voting is a right and duty. The remaining questions permit a rather more personal or subjective reaction. However, it is not our purpose here to solve the puzzles produced by the experiment in questionnaire format. For purposes of detecting change, it is more to the point to inquire whether the estimate of change depends upon which form of the 1971 interview is involved. Fortunately, it turns out that the change is in the same direction using either Form A or Form B. The magnitude of the contextual effect is, however, a reminder of the uncertainty as to the exact size of the change.

As was noted, the statements on voting seem to tap the respondent's endorsement of a particular norm concerning the citizen's role. It is interesting, therefore, that there is fairly little change in frequency of agreement with statements 1 and 4. What change does appear, however, is in the direction of a weakened affirmation of the desirability of voting.

The remaining four statements in Table 40 all suggest a decrease in the sense of political efficacy. We feel particularly confident of this estimate of the direction of change for questions 2 and 3, since there are two different base-line readings on them—each, no doubt, subject to its own sources of contextual variation. It is unfortunate, however, that the comparisons between 1957 and 1971 are somewhat artificial, in that only two response alternatives, agree and disagree, were available in 1957, and we sought to match these by combining strongly agree with agree and strongly disagree with disagree in the 1971 data. Despite such difficulties there is no real reason to doubt the major thrust of the findings: the 1971 respondents do express a less confident attitude about the extent to which the political process responds to their needs than did the 1957 or 1954 respondents. Indeed, the extent to which public officials are seen as unresponsive (questions 5 and 6) is really quite startling, in the light of the response distributions obtained in 1954 and 1957. Granting uncertainties due to extraneous sources of response variation, we can only conclude that these data reflect a serious erosion of the citizen's confidence in the intentions of those elected to serve and govern him.

Racial Attitudes

Although the years 1952 to 1959 were important from the standpoint of American race relations, national surveys of racial attitudes and beliefs were rare during that period.[1] This is equally true for the Detroit Area Study, which included only a handful of such questions addressed to whites and none at all specifically to blacks. Perhaps this is an instance where the absence of questions itself constitutes a social indicator of the degree of concern or lack of concern over a social problem.

All told, we located only four DAS questions from the 1950s for replication, two from 1956 and two from 1958. However, in 1968 an entire study was done on black racial attitudes, and in 1969 a study focused on white racial attitudes.[2] Despite the brief interval, we repeated questions in 1971 from each of these surveys, though mainly from the 1968 black study where the possibility of change seemed greater and was less well documented elsewhere.

One note of caution is needed: since the comparable black sample sizes in 1968 and 1971 were only 600 and 342 respectively, differences large enough to be considered reliable elsewhere in this report may not be statistically significant here. We continue to indicate non-significance where it is not fairly obvious. Another issue of interest is

[1] A National Opinion Research Center set of questions on white racial attitudes in 1956 constitutes an important exception. See Paul B. Sheatsley, "White Attitudes Toward the Negro," *Daedalus* (Winter, 1966): 217–238. More recent NORC data to 1970 are incorporated into Andrew M. Greeley and Paul B. Sheatsley, "Attitudes Toward Racial Integration," *Scientific American* (December 1971): 13–19. See also Mildred A. Schwartz, *Trends in White Attitudes Toward Negroes*, National Opinion Research Center, 1967, and for a different and later set of trend data, Angus Campbell, *White Attitudes Toward Black People*, Institute for Social Research, 1971, Chapter 7.

[2] The 1968 Detroit Area Study (some data from which are here reported for the first time) was supported in part by a grant to Howard Schuman from the National Institute of Mental Health (MH 15537).

that concerning the race of the interviewers, since previous research indicates that black attitudinal responses are affected by this factor. Both black and white interviewers were employed for black respondents in 1968 and in 1971, and results have been standardized for the two years by computing them separately for each race of interviewer and then taking the unweighted average.[3] We have elsewhere worked with the results for black interviewers alone, and it is interesting to note that while the amount of change varies somewhat between the two analyses, broad conclusions based on significance and non-significance are virtually identical. A few interviews with white respondents were taken by black interviewers in 1971 (less than 4 percent); although some race-of-interviewer effects are apparent, they do not change the major findings reported here.

RACIAL ATTITUDES OF WHITES

Our findings of change from the 1950s show the same large and significant trends toward liberalization of white attitudes that have been reported elsewhere. Two items from 1958 are presented in Table 41, one dealing with separate schooling, the other with residential integration. The first shows a 17 percent shift from 1958 to 1971 in approval of integrated schools; the second an even larger change of 28 percent toward acceptance of at least token residential integration.

The school item probably does not have the same meaning today that it had in 1958. In the earlier year the focus of public debate was almost entirely on the South, but by mid-1971 the issues of de facto segregation in Northern schools and of prospective two-way busing were already salient for cities like Detroit. We cannot disentangle changes in question meaning from changes in underlying attitude, but it may be that the difference on the school

[3] For further details and other adjustments made to effect comparability, see Howard Schuman, *Trends and Complexities in Black Racial Attitudes,* Institute for Social Research, University of Michigan (forthcoming).

Table 41. School and Neighborhood Integration (White Respondents)

Personally, do you think white students and Negro students should go to the same schools, or to separate schools?	*Percent Distribution*	
	1958	*1971*
Same schools	62	79
Unsure	6	4
Separate schools	33	17
	100	100
Would you be at all disturbed or unhappy if a Negro with the same income and education as you moved into your block?		
Yes	54	28
Unsure	6	4
No	40	68
	100	100

question is the smallest of the long-term shifts we examine in this section because of this alteration in meaning. The residential question, on the other hand, retained much the same interpretation in 1971 that it had in 1958, though the actual amount of such minimal housing integration, as described in the question, may have increased slightly in the Detroit area over the thirteen-year period. Since the housing issue is still a vital one, the movement from majority reservations against such integration to two-thirds acceptance of it represents an important change in white sentiments.

The "playmate question" shown in Table 42 concerns an area of interpersonal relations which is not so well-defined as a national political issue; the question was devised by Angell and his co-workers in the 1956 study to get at what they called "moral norms" in the area of race relations.[4] Overall, the difference between 1956 and 1971 is 39 percentage points—a massive change in personal atti-

[4] Robert C. Angell, "Preferences for Moral Norms in Three Problem Areas," *American Journal of Sociology,* 67 (May 1962): 650–660.

Table 42. Play Between Black and White Children
(White Respondents)

One day a six year old asks her mother if she can bring another girl home to play. The mother knows that the other girl is a Negro, and that her own daughter has only played with white children before. What should the mother do?	*Percent Distribution*			
	1956	*1971*	*1969*[a]	*1971*[a]
1. She should tell her daughter she must never play with Negroes;	13	3	2	2
2. The daughter should be told that she may play with Negro children in school, but not at home;	47	18	22	17
3. The Negro child should be permitted to come to the home.	40	79	76	81
	100	100	100	100

[a] Heads of household and spouses only, 21–69 years of age.

tudes or public values, as the case may be. In 1956 the majority of the white Detroit population discouraged easy relations between black and white children, but in 1971 four out of five white adults claimed to be willing to encourage at least one kind of friendly tie between such children. That the change has not yet run its course is suggested by the 1969–1971 comparison: within the space of just two years a small but significant increase of 4 percent was registered. Although this question may seem almost patronizing to some readers today, the magnitude of the public transformation deserves emphasis.

Moreover, white adults are themselves conscious to a considerable extent of the change they have experienced. Asked in 1971 how would you "have answered this question about 15 years ago," only 57 percent chose the "home" response, while 18 percent reported that "never play" would have been their answer. Altogether, 69 percent of the respondents indicated that their view of the matter was the same in 1956 as in 1971, while 29 percent were aware of having become more favorable toward racial contact and

2 percent were aware of having become less favorable. These results suggest that some persons whose attitudes actually changed were not aware that this was happening or, if aware, were unwilling to acknowledge that their attitudes formerly were different. However, awareness of change at the individual level is quite widespread relative to the actual magnitude of the change.

Many writers have emphasized that white racial attitudes and practices in America have always had a large element of mass conformity. Since race itself is a visible characteristic, racial interaction is easily observed and readily subjected to social sanctions. For this reason it is interesting to determine the degree of support attitude holders believe themselves to have from their social environment. We have fragmentary data on this from 1956, and more precise data from 1971. Table 43 shows that in 1956 those who themselves said "never play with Negroes" generally believed that "most people in Detroit" would agree with them, while those who encouraged integrated play in

Table 43. Beliefs About the Attitudes of Others on Playmate Question (White Respondents)

Do you think that most people in the Detroit area would agree with you on what should be done about this?	*Percent Distribution*	
	1956	*1971*
[Among those who themselves say "never play"]		
Yes	88	54
No	12	46
	100	100
[Among those who themselves say "home"]		
Yes	31	35
No	69	65
	100	100
[What most people in Detroit are believed to respond]		
Never play	. . .	17
School only	. . .	51
Home	. . .	32
		100

their homes tended to see themselves in the minority. The latter perception continued to hold in 1971, but now those who said "never play" also were much less sure of public support for their position. (The number of cases involved in these comparisons is small, but the difference over time for the "never play" category is quite reliable.) Exactly what is going on in the later year becomes somewhat clearer if we focus on the 1971 study, where an additional question provides a picture of Detroit opinion on the play-mate issue as perceived by *all respondents taken together*. According to our respondents' beliefs, the "play at school only" alternative is the dominant public position, although in fact this was not the case, as we saw earlier in Table 42. Thus, public opinion on this racial issue is in advance of what the public *believes* to be public opinion. Moreover, while many are aware of their own changes in attitude, as previously noted, there is a lag in recognition of the collective shift in attitudes.

This exhausts the items available from base-line studies in the 1950s, but Table 44 provides findings from 1969 and 1971 for a question on intermarriage. The issue can scarcely be termed one of much practical significance, given the extremely low rate of racial intermarriage in the United States, but it represents a symbolic point of some import. Not only has intermarriage been a traditional bug-aboo of race relations, but it constitutes perhaps the best verbal indicator available of complete acceptance by whites of equal status for blacks. Neither in 1969 nor in 1971 was this step accepted freely by many in the white population. But it is of some note that in the space of just two years, there is evidence for a visible (and significant) liberalization even on this sensitive question. In 1969, two-thirds of the white population responded in terms of minding intermarriage "a lot"; in 1971, the fraction had dropped to one-half.

In summary, all evidence reviewed here on white attitudes points to a large and continuing shift toward acceptance of principles of equal treatment and equal status for black Americans. Yet it is possible that our focus in this

Table 44. Intermarriage

White Respondents[a]	Percent Distribution	
If a very close relative married a Negro, would you mind it	1969	1971
a lot	68	51
a little, or	18	29
not at all?	15	20
	100	100

Black Respondents[a]		
Suppose a very close relative married a white person. Would you mind it		
a lot	. . .	7
a little, or	. . .	9
not at all?	. . .	84
		100

[a] Heads of household and spouses only, 21–69 years of age.

report on change may produce too optimistic a picture. In particular, black Americans reading these pages today may be struck as much by the distance still to travel as by the distance already traversed. Some hint of this is provided by black responses in 1971 to the complementary question on intermarriage, also shown in Table 44. The gulf between black and white acceptance of such cross-race marriage is vast: 84 percent vs. 20 percent. The gulf is not difficult to understand in historical terms, but awareness of its size may help us understand some of the findings, presented subsequently, on black attitudes.

One other question asked only in 1971 shows a good deal more convergence in black and white answers: to an inquiry on whether "intermarriage between whites and Negroes will eventually come to be accepted by most Americans," 81 percent of the black sample and 61 percent of the white sample responded yes. This was the only question in the study that asked for a forecast of future social changes. It appears that in venturing such forecasts, respondents are in some measure aware of current trends. At least, this particular forecast amounts to an extrapolation of the actual trend as we infer it from the 1969 and 1971 surveys.

RACIAL ATTITUDES OF BLACKS

The 1968 survey of black attitudes took place less than a year after the major Detroit riot of 1967, and black respondents were asked a question about the effects of the riot on white attitudes. When we repeated the question in approximately the same form in 1971, there was an increase of 13 percent in the proportion who believed the riot had turned whites against equal rights (Table 45). Whether through reflection or subsequent experience, black adults in Detroit took a significantly more negative view of the consequences of the riot in 1971 than they had in 1968.

Table 45. Effects of the 1967 Detroit Riot (Black Respondents)

(1968) Do you think that because of the disturbance there are more whites in favor of equal rights for Negroes, fewer whites in favor, or that there isn't much difference?

(1971) This next question deals with the effects of the riot in Detroit four years ago in July, 1967. Do you think that because of that disturbance there are more whites in favor of equal rights for Negroes, fewer whites in favor, or that the riot didn't make much difference?[a]

	Percent Distribution	
	1968	1971
More whites	53	42
Fewer whites	9	22
Not much difference	38	36
	100	100

[a] The introductory first sentence added in 1971 was not necessary in 1968 because the latter survey had preceded the question with several others on the 1967 riot, including one about the term "riot" itself. Both the 1968 and 1971 studies instructed interviewers to substitute for "Negro" the term "black" (or some other term) if the respondent indicated such a preference.

The 1967 riot was of course a single historical event, albeit an extremely important one. There is the larger question of whether black beliefs about white attitudes have changed in a more general way since 1968. As we saw above, white attitudes have liberalized appreciably since the 1950s, and even noticeably since 1969. Despite this, Table 46 shows that black skepticism about white attitudes has been growing. Over the 1968–1971 time span, the proportion of blacks who say that they trust no whites increased from 6 percent to 10 percent, and the proportion believing that most whites want to keep blacks down rose from 18 to 27 percent. These opposing racial trends can perhaps be understood at least in part by recognizing that white attitudes and actions are still far from complete racial tolerance, while black expectations for a total societal transformation are accelerating at a rapid rate. But whatever the interpretation, the increased, or increasingly open, black distrust of white intentions is an important factor in American race relations.

The questions just discussed deal with the presumed inner states of white people as inferred by blacks. When we turn to black beliefs about more concrete acts of discrimination, the evidence of change is more mixed, as shown in Table 47. There is practically no change at all in

Table 46. Black Beliefs About White Intentions

On the whole, do you think most white people in Detroit want	*Percent Distribution*	
	1968	*1971*
to see Negroes get a better break,	48	37
or do they want to keep Negroes down,	18	27
or don't they care one way or the other?	33	36
	100	100
Do you personally feel that you can trust		
most white people,	21	13
some white people,	73	78
or none at all?	6	10
	100	100 ·

the percentage of blacks who see a difference between black and white teachers in their interest in black children. A small increase occurs in the proportion believing that discrimination in hiring is pervasive, but the difference is not large enough to be reliable. The same is true of more general black beliefs about discrimination: the change between 1968 and 1971 is in the direction of greater skepticism about progress in the elimination of discrimination, but the difference is too slight to reach significance. Only

Table 47. Black Beliefs About Discrimination

	Percent Distribution	
Do you think Negro teachers take more of an interest in teaching Negro students than white teachers do?	1968	1971
Yes	34	35
No	66	65
	100	100
How many places in Detroit do you think will hire a white person before they will hire a Negro even though they have the same qualifications?		
Many	56	60
Some	23	20
Few	20	20
	100	100
Some people say that over the last 10 or 15 years, there has been a lot of progress in getting rid of racial discrimination. Others say there hasn't been much real change for most Negroes over that time. Which do you agree with most?		
Lot of progress	73	69
No real change	27	31
	100	100
Do you think Negro customers who shop in the big downtown stores are treated as politely as white customers, or are they treated less politely?		
As politely	74	64
Less politely	26	36
	100	100

for one specific belief—that store clerks discriminate against black customers—is there a reliable increase between 1968 and 1971. Why this one question shows a more pronounced change is not clear, but it seems improbable that it reflects an actual increase in discrimination in this area. Possibly it results from increased use of downtown Detroit stores by a larger number of blacks, as a consequence of the increase in black numbers and proportion in the central city. Or there may be increasing black sensitivity to subtle signs of lack of respect that were once accepted more passively. In any case, this is the only specific item on discrimination that shows the same reliable change over time that was indicated earlier for more general beliefs about white attitudes.

To this point we have focused on what blacks believe about whites. At least equally important are black goals and means to reaching those goals. In the 1950s the emphasis of black leadership was on "integration," but by the later 1960s terms like "black power," "community control," and "black consciousness" received increasing attention at the national level. The 1968 DAS included several questions on these topics, and three were repeated in 1971. All three show shifts (Table 48) toward increasing "black consciousness," though only in one case is this large enough to register as significant. This one instance involves preference for all black or mostly black neighborhoods, a choice which rose from 7 to 15 percent over the three-year span. The change is made somewhat ambiguous by the complexity of the question format and the fact that the compensating decrease comes from a volunteered rather than precoded category. If we take the results in Table 48 literally, it appears that blacks are "dividing up" more sharply, for the proportion opting for a "mixed" neighborhood rises nearly as much as that choosing an essentially black residential setting. The decrease comes among those inclined to treat race as a wholly irrelevant factor—a category that drops sharply from 32 to 17 percent.

A question on black principals for all-black schools shows a slightly greater emphasis on black community

Table 48. Black Power and Black Consciousness

Would you personally prefer to live in a neighborhood with all Negroes, mostly Negroes, mostly whites, or a neighborhood that's mixed half and half?	Percent Distribution	
	1968	1971
All Negroes	4	7
Mostly Negroes	3	8
Mostly Whites	2	2
Mixed	59	66
Makes no difference (Volunteered)	32	17
	100	100
Some people say there should be Negro principals in schools with mostly Negro students because Negroes should have the most say in running inner-city schools? Would you agree with that or not?		
Yes	35	39
No	65	61
	100	100
On another subject (related to how you spend your spare time), could you tell me who two or three of your favorite actors or entertainers are? [Coded for race of each entertainer mentioned][a]		
All black	29	30
Majority blacks	21	24
Half black/half white	13	9
Majority white	21	22
All white	17	15
	100	100

[a] In 1968 all names given were coded; in 1971 only the first three names were coded.

control, but the difference fails to reach significance. Nor should we assume too quickly that the apparent shift is real even though small, for we shall shortly note a difference as large as this one but in an unexpected direction.

A more indirect question on black cultural consciousness invited respondents to name their favorite actors or entertainers. These names were classified by race during the later coding stage of the project. Table 48 shows a slight tendency for black names to increase in mention, but the difference is not significant, nor altogether clear in direction. The 1971 figures in Table 48 actually comprise two versions of the question: one given to half the respondents before other racial questions were asked, the other given at the end of a series of race-related items. The latter variation might have been expected to stimulate black respondents to increase their mention of black entertainers, but in fact no such difference emerges. Taken together with the other two questions in Table 48, we must conclude that the evidence for a growing allegiance to the concept of black consciousness in the Detroit community is not very strong, though of course the period of time covered by our two surveys is brief. That fairly rapid cultural change is certainly possible along some lines is shown by a question on racial self-designation asked only in 1971: 42 percent of the sample chose "black" or "Afro-American" (in preference to "Negro" or "colored") although it can reasonably be assumed that that figure would have been close to zero less than a decade earlier. Our evidence does not, of course, speak to the question of what changes in behavior might follow from an enhancement of black consciousness—if, indeed, that is the meaning of these responses.

If the rejection of integration as a viable goal was one major racial theme of the late sixties, the rejection of nonviolence as an adequate means to equal rights was the other. Changes along the second line are shown in Table 49. For analysis of the first question in that table, the two "non-violent" alternatives were collapsed, since other analysis indicated that they were not distinguishable from one another in terms of implication; the two together were then tested against the third response ("violence"). The difference is significant, although it is much less striking in magnitude than for the second question on violence, where this line of action is heavily qualified by being made contingent on prior failure of other means. Together the two questions suggest that violence is a first choice for only a tiny segment of the black population, but that when pressed, many more black respondents are willing to agree that it

Table 49. Opinions on Use of Violence (Black Respondents)

As you see it, what's the best way for Negroes to try to gain their rights	Percent Distribution	
	1968	*1971*
use laws and persuasion,	30	39
use non-violent protest,	64	49
or be ready to use violence?	6	11
	100	100
[Asked only of those not saying violence to preceding question] If (laws and persuasion/non-violent protest) doesn't work, then do you think Negroes should be ready to use violence?		
Yes	22	44
No	78	56
	100	100

may ultimately be necessary to call on violence to combat racial injustice. The reader is cautioned to take account of these qualifications in question wording, lest the import of the findings be exaggerated.

The results thus far show changes toward greater distrust of whites, increased preference for black association, and some second thoughts on traditional techniques of non-violence for achieving equal rights. Along with quite reliable differences over time on several items are a number of non-significant differences which may appear to show smaller supporting shifts for other attitudes. If one attempts to assimilate all the differences to a single grand theme, one might be tempted to talk of the greater alienation of the black population, its total dis-identification with the United States. Such a conclusion would lead to the expectation that when blacks are asked a broad question on willingness to defend America, many would say no—and certainly more in 1971 than in 1968. In fact, we asked, "If our country got into a big World War today, would you personally feel the United States is worth fighting for?" and found that the proportion of black respondents unwilling to fight for the United States in a major war was quite small in both years; it actually declined (non-significantly) from 13 percent in 1968 to 8 percent in 1971. The evidence is that the separate strands of black disenchantment with white society do not add up to a total rejection of the United States, at least as measured by this one question. The interpretation of any single item in isolation is hazardous, but we must count ourselves warned against too sweeping a conclusion about black alienation on the basis of the several findings reported in this section.

The Complexity of Social Change

This report contains no summary chapter. We want to explain why this omission seems like a wise decision since the statement of our reasons may contain instructive cautions.

First, we were deliberately eclectic in our selection of topics, so that we would be able to give as many diverse illustrations as possible of the strategy of measuring change via replication of base-line surveys. Although the design of the study does not reflect an attempt to develop a comprehensive or unified theory of social change, we fear that post hoc interpretation of our results will be all too easy for anyone already persuaded of the power of such a theory. Thus, if one believes that the master trend in American society is expressed by the notion of bureaucratization, each of the changes we described will be interpreted as an instance of increased involvement in or dependence upon bureaucracies, or else as a reaction, favorable or unfavorable, to the bureaucratic trend. Without taking issue with this or any other special interpretation of the course of social change, we would like to illustrate the difficulty in reaching rigorous inferences about the causal processes underlying the diverse kinds of change revealed by our data.

The basic reason for the difficulty can be stated as a general principle: the fact that two variables change together is no proof that they are causally related. Not only does covariation over time fail to prove that one variable causes the other; it need not even imply that they depend on the same causes or that both are reflections of some common underlying process of change. Thus, when we report that changes in two or more items are "consistent" as to their indication of what change is occurring, we are already engaged in a causal inference that goes beyond the data. All such statements in this report are merely causal *hypotheses* requiring further investigation, analysis, or theoretical support before they can be accepted as findings.

An illustration of the logical hazard is at hand. In Figure 7 we have juxtaposed our data on change in two items, the question on whether the United States should intervene in a South American revolution and the question on whether a child should be allowed to bring home a black playmate. As we have already reported, these questions reveal a shift toward a position of non-intervention in the affairs of a South American nation and toward a more tolerant attitude about association between persons of different racial groups. Both changes are pronounced and occur over the same fifteen-year period (although if we had data for other years, we might find that the changes

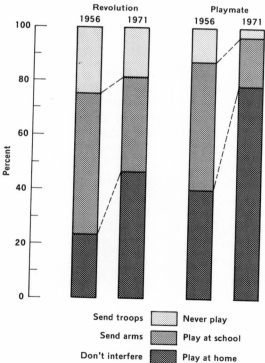

Figure 7. Changes in Responses to Revolution and Playmate Questions (Percent Distributions for White Respondents) 1956 to 1971. (Note: See Tables 37 and 42 for wording of questions.)

were not completely synchronous). An analyst seeking some theme to tie the two questions together might suggest that the population is shifting toward the liberal pole of a general, underlying dimension of conservative versus liberal ideologies which is reflected in attitudes toward both foreign affairs (treating non-intervention as a "liberal" position) and race relations (regarding freedom of association between racial groups as a "liberal" position). But without prejudice to such a thesis as a general proposition, we would have to point out that it is quite implausible as an explanation of the particular coincidental changes in these data. Our evidence is that in neither year was the response to the playmate question correlated significantly with the response to the revolution question (Table 50).

Table 50. Responses (Percent Distribution for White Respondents) to Playmate Question, by Responses to Revolution Question, in 1956 and 1971

		Playmate Question			
Year	Revolution Question	Never Play	Play at School	Play at Home	Total
1956	Send troops	16	44	40	100
	Send arms	8	52	40	100
	Don't interfere	15	45	40	100
1971	Send troops	4	22	75	100
	Send arms	3	18	79	100
	Don't interfere	3	17	81	100

Note: See Tables 37 and 42 for wording of questions. Chi-square test shows no significant association between the two questions in either year.

Now, it is logically possible, despite the finding just reported, that there was some connection between the *changes* in answers to the two questions, even though responses to the two questions are unrelated both at the beginning and at the end of the time period. However, it is possible to show by a mathematical argument (which will not be reproduced here) that it would require a very unusual configuration of the data for this to be true, so unusual in fact that *no* simple explanation (such as that offered by our hypothetical analyst) would be consistent with the data.

Another example of changes occurring together relates to the follow-up to the playmate and revolution questions: Do you think most people in Detroit would agree with you on this? For each question there was a decrease between 1956 and 1971 in the proportion believing their opinion commands majority support. Hence, the analyst might infer an increasing general willingness of respondents to endorse what they believe to be minority views, or an increasing uncertainty of respondents about the normative legitimacy of their own opinions, or some other common cause of a shift in the perception of how other people's opinions resemble one's own. Again, the interpretation would not be supported merely by the coincidental timing of shifts on the two questions. But, contrary to the earlier illustration, there would be support from the fact that, in both 1956 and 1971, if the respondent believed he was in the majority on the revolution question, then he was more likely to have the same belief in regard to the playmate question (see Table 51). Indeed, a chi-square test suggests that the association between the two questions was just as strong in one year as in the other.

Table 51. Belief that Most People Would Agree on Playmate Question by Belief They Would Agree on Revolution Question (Percent Distribution for White Respondents) in 1956 and 1971

Year	Revolution[a] Question: Would most people agree?	Playmate[a] Question: Would most people agree?		Total
		Yes	No	
1956	Yes (85%)	62	38	100
	No (15%)	41	59	100
	Total (100%)	59	41	100
1971	Yes (67%)	46	54	100
	No (33%)	32	68	100
	Total (100%)	41	59	100

[a] See Tables 37, 42, and 43 for wording of questions.

If we then inquire more closely into the distribution of the belief that one is siding with the majority, we find that the pattern is different for the revolution and playmate questions. In 1956, five-sixths of all respondents thought that most other Detroiters agreed with them on the revolution question, whatever their own views on this question (see Table 52). But in the same year, those taking the most liberal position on the playmate question accurately perceived that they were not in the majority, while those taking the least liberal position were overwhelmingly convinced that their position was the majority one, even though people sharing this view were a distinct minority. These relationships changed decidedly between 1956 and 1971. On the revolution question, the actual opinions (Figure 7) had shifted toward the non-intervention position. Those continuing to hold the interventionist view ("send troops") were much more ready to concede that their view did not command the majority position, while those in the non-

Table 52. Belief that Most People in Detroit Would Agree, by Respondent's Answer to Playmate and Revolution Questions (White Respondents)

	Would most people agree? (Percent "Yes")	
Respondent's answer	1956	1971
Revolution question		
Send troops	83	49
Send arms	88	63
Don't interfere	82	78
All answers	85	67
Playmate question		
Never play	89	51
Play at school	75	69
Play at home	31	35
All answers	59	41

Note: See Tables 37, 42, and 43 for wording of questions. Some percentages in this table differ slightly from corresponding figures in Table 43, since only respondents giving classifiable answers to both the revolution and playmate questions are included here.

interventionist camp, by and large, continued to be convinced that theirs was the one preferred by most Detroiters. By contrast, on the playmate question, although the most liberal answer did in fact command a decisive majority in 1971, hardly more than a third of those adopting this position believed that it was the one preferred by other Detroiters. Yet, those holding the least liberal view realistically had become much less certain than they were in 1956 that they were in the majority. Actually, it was the intermediate category ("play at school") whose adherents, in 1971, were most likely to believe that other Detroit people were with them on this question.

We have to conclude, in short, that the perception that one shares the majority view on a given question is a complicated one. The perception evidently depends on one's own opinion, but the nature of that dependence may change in different ways over time. Hence, even though the perception that one is in the majority on one question is associated with the same perception on an unrelated question, we cannot explain the similarity of the changes in these perceptions by the same processes. Here, we have shown that whatever explanation may be ventured will have to be somewhat more complicated than the mere hypothesis that people are increasingly willing to adopt what they think is a minority view on all questions.

The caution against premature inferences about causal relationships between concomitant changes revealed by this study can be stated more broadly. We have not, of course, described all the changes going on in the Detroit area between the 1950s and 1971. Most readers will be aware of such changes as the rise in levels of real income in this population, improvements in educational attainment, the shifting racial composition of the population, the relocation of the population toward the suburban ring, and many other social, economic, demographic, and political changes. Although we cannot present the evidence here, we do have reason to doubt that many of the changes in attitudes, norms, values, and behavior that we have described can be accounted for in any substantial way by shifts in the makeup of the Detroit area population or by the turnover due to in- and out-migration. To be sure, in our further work we hope to offer precise estimates of the contribution of such shifts to the changes presented here and to engage in further analysis and theoretical discussion of the interrelations of changes of all kinds. Our message is simply that this will be a long and arduous task, not to be accomplished merely by the exercise of the sociological imagination.

As an alternative to a summary that would offer a unified theoretical interpretation of all the changes revealed by our data—an impossible task, we believe, in the present state of knowledge—we might have attempted a summary that tries to make a compact evaluation of the entire set of changes. If we could classify each change as desirable or undesirable in terms of its meaning for or impact upon the general population, we might then sum up the plusses and minuses to reach an overall judgment as to whether the changes represent improvement or deterioration in the quality of life. No doubt some readers will, in effect, make such judgments from their own personal perspectives. Occasionally, social scientists too have entertained the possibility of providing some general assessment of social progress or retrogression in the form of an aggregated index that would inform us if welfare or illfare is, on the whole, increasing or decreasing. But, as the authors of *Toward a Social Report* concluded, "the goal of a grand and cosmic measure of all forms or aspects of welfare must be dismissed as impractical, for the present at any rate."[1]

A possible alternative to a synthetic, arithmetically aggregated index, would be a selection of questions inviting respondents, in effect, to provide their own general evaluations of the drift of events and affairs. We do have a few questions that we interpret as possible reflections of the morale of the population and that seem to imply rather global assessments of the course of social change.

[1] U.S. Department of Health, Education, and Welfare, *Toward a Social Report*, Washington: U.S. Government Printing Office, 1969, p. 99.

The question broached in Table 53, concerning the respondent's estimate of the chances of war with one of America's international rivals, yields results contrary to the remainder of our report; for between 1959 and 1971 there was an appreciable increase in the proportion thinking a war with Russia in the next quarter of a century

Table 53. Likelihood of Atomic War with Russia

What would you say are the chances that the United States will be in an atomic war with Russia in the next 25 years?	Percent Distribution		
	1958[a]	1959	1971
Certain	5	5	2
More likely than not	26	8	6
Chances about 50–50	9	26	21
Some chance	31	41	40
No chance at all	15	14	26
Don't know	14	6	5
	100	100	100

[a] In 1958, the question was open-ended; responses were recorded in the respondent's own words and then coded to categories approximating these. In both 1959 and 1971 the respondent was asked to choose among the first five alternatives.

quite unlikely. (The 1958 data are not really comparable, for the reason noted in the footnote, but are included to remind the reader how important it is, in trying to estimate change, to secure as close an approximation as possible to exact replication.) So far as these data go, they suggest some increment of optimism about what has hitherto been a significant source of anxiety for the public. What the data do not speak to, however, is the question of whether other sources of possible armed conflict have come to seem more probable as the danger of hostilities with Russia has seemingly receded.

By contrast with the outlook for war with Russia, another historic anxiety—the likelihood of another great depression—seems to have become more salient since 1959; there was an increment of about 10 percentage points in the proportion anticipating such a depression "some day" (see number 4, Table 54). We do not know, of course, whether this estimate of the long-run prospect is really affected quite strongly by short-run ups and downs in economic conditions and outlook. Further replications of this question—and, really, a similar remark applies to almost all our questions—will be needed to determine whether the change from a particular point in the 1950s to 1971 is indicative of a persistent trend or merely reflects transitory circumstances.

Three questions in Table 54 (2, 3, and 6) are phrased in terms of very general optimistic or pessimistic reactions to the respondent's estimate of prospects for the future. A valuable feature of the pair of questions, 2 and 6, is that they have opposite wordings, so that a consistently optimistic respondent should agree that children have a wonderful future (2) but disagree with the statement that it is hardly fair to bring children into the world (6). In point of fact, not all respondents are consistent in their responses to these questions, or, for that matter, to any other pair of questions that seem to measure the same attitude. But if, as some students of attitude measurement believe, questions of this kind are contaminated by an "agreeing response tendency," then we can feel more confident of our conclusion as to change when the two items yield the same conclusion about the change. In fact, both questions about the future, as it relates to children in particular, reveal an increase in pessimism between 1958 and 1971. The conclusion is even stronger for statement 6, since there are three independent base-line measurements from the late 1950s. Question 3 shows a more ambiguous result. When the 1956 and 1958 surveys are used for the base-line measurement, the change in the pessimistic direction is significant. The 1959 survey, with the question in a slightly different format, produced a response distribution similar to that obtained in 1971.

Items 1 and 5 in Table 54 and the two questions in Table 55 treat optimism and pessimism, not in the temporal dimension, but in terms of the trust or confidence one can have in his fellow man. Of these four questions, only

Table 54. Morale Items

| | | Percent Distribution | | | |
		Agree	Unsure	Dis-agree	Total
1. Most people don't really	1956	34	<1	66	100
care what happens to	1958	34	3	63	100
the next fellow	1971	50	4	46	100
	1971[a]	52	1	47	100
2. Children born today	1958	79	9	12	100
have a wonderful future	1971	50	11	39	100
to look forward to					
3. Nowadays a person has	1956	26	1	73	100
to live pretty much for	1958	31	3	66	100
today and let tomorrow	1959[b]	37	. . .	63	100
take care of itself	1971	39	3	58	100
	1971[a]	40	1	59	100
4. The chances are very	1959[b]	39	. . .	61	100
good that some day	1971	46	9	45	100
we'll have another	1971[a]	49	3	48	100
depression as bad as					
the one in the thirties					
5. These days a person	1956	58	1	41	100
doesn't really know	1958	64	3	33	100
whom he can count on	1959[b]	52	. . .	48	100
	1971	62	4	34	100
	1971[a]	64	1	35	100
6. It's hardly fair to bring	1956	13	1	86	100
children into the world	1958	11	7	82	100
the way things look for	1959[b]	20	. . .	80	100
the future	1971	35	5	60	100
	1971[a]	36	1	63	100

[a] After probe (to simulate comparability with 1956 data).
[b] 1959 response categories (strongly agree, agree, disagree, and strongly disagree) have been collapsed.

statement 5 fails to show a substantial and unambiguous change in the pessimistic direction. The equivocal outcome of this item, "These days a person doesn't really know whom he can count on," due to the discrepant results for different inter-year comparisons and question formats, warns us that there is always the chance of non-negligible

Table 55. Confidence in Human Nature

Would you say that most people are more inclined to help others, or are they more inclined to look out for themselves?	Percent Distribution	
	1959	*1971*
Help others	32	17
Look out for themselves	63	79
It depends	5	4
	100	100
In general, do you think that most people can be trusted, or do you feel that a person can't be too careful in his dealings with others?		
Most can be trusted	48	37
Can't be too careful	46	59
It depends	6	4
	100	100

measurement error in these crude attempts to assess the direction of change in attitudes. Still, the bulk of our evidence points to a reduction of confidence in human nature. In 1956 and 1958, one-third of the respondents agreed that most people don't really care what happens to the next fellow; in 1971, agreement had risen to one-half. Between 1959 and 1971, the proportion feeling that most people can be trusted declined from 48 to 37 percent. In 1959, one-third of the sample felt that most people are inclined to help others rather than look out for themselves; in 1971, only one-sixth were this trusting of their fellow human beings.

The ethic of responsibility requires that the authors refrain from broad interpretations of these results not warranted by the data themselves or other adequate evidence. Having been part of the research apparatus that generated the statistics, perhaps we have as lively an appreciation of their fallibility as anyone can. We hope that our presentation has been sufficiently impartial that the reader may draw his own conclusions without being unduly influenced by any biases we may have communicated. It is to be expected that readers will differ in their interpretations. Indeed, one of the more worthwhile contributions to which we could aspire would be the stimulation of debate about the meaning and implications of the trends we have discerned. For what it is worth, we can record, in conclusion, some of the public reaction to the material on morale that has just been presented. Some of these data were released to the press in July 1972. One small-town paper headed an editorial, "Are Attitudes Eroding?" which concluded:

> These surveys are interesting for what they reveal about attitudes. How accurately they reflect the feelings of the total population, of course, nobody knows. The part which is worrisome is that which indicates an erosion of values as we have known them, the growth of indifference toward others and preoccupation with the present.

In another small town, the editor queried, "To care or not to care, that is the question." He felt that local participation in the Red Cross mobile blood clinic was so high as to suggest that more people care in his community than in metropolitan Detroit.

In a somewhat larger city, the editor read us as depicting "a cold, cynical world" and offered his diagnosis:

> Perhaps the prime reason for this isolation is the increasing complexity of our economic and social systems, resulting in bureaucracies insensitive to citizens, unions insensitive to their rank and file, and businesses insensitive to both customer and employe. This, of course, is a blanket indictment which does not apply to every government official, labor leader, or businessman. But the depersonalization of our institutions is the chief problem we must deal with.

Finally, we should like to quote the editor in a medium-sized city who summarized our results under the heading, "Some Disturbing Thoughts," and concluded:

> Sociologists will be spending the next year or so determining what these and other apparent trends really mean. But the raw data gives the layman a pretty good idea right now.

Acknowledgements

This study was made possible by funding from Russell Sage Foundation to the University of Michigan, supplementing the University's regular budget for the Detroit Area Study (DAS) so as to support a study sufficiently large to replicate several base-line studies. We wish to pay tribute to the work of Eleanor Bernert Sheldon, formerly of Russell Sage Foundation, in directing the Foundation's program, Studies of Social Change. Our project is but one of many stimulated and supported by that impressive program.

There could have been no study of social change like ours had there not been base-line studies to replicate. It would be difficult to overstate our indebtedness to the research workers who carried out the nine base-line studies we used. On the average, some thirty students and two faculty participants were involved in each of those studies. Their names are listed in *The Detroit Area Study: A Description and Bibliography of Materials Based on Detroit Area Study Research, September 1, 1951—June 30, 1969,* a brochure published in July 1969 by DAS. The reader who would like to gain a sense of what is involved in this kind of research enterprise may request a copy of that brochure from The Detroit Area Study, LSA Building, The University of Michigan, Ann Arbor 48104.

In the 1971 survey we depended heavily on the efforts of Laurie Vander Velde, Secretary of DAS, and Jon Entin, Elizabeth Fischer, Frank Munger, and Linda Romagnoli, Teaching Fellows. The student participants were: Stephen M. Aigner, Sunny Bradford, Alan Connor, Solomon Davis, Hasan Dogan, Barry Edmonston, Mark Evers, Robert J. Fournier, Phil Gleason, Robert M. Groves, Robert L. Hampton, Shirley J. Hatchett, Robert A. Johnson, Toni Martin, James McClure, Kristin R. A. Moore, John R. Pfeiffer, Daisy Quarm, Greg Rodd, Emilie Schmeidler, Richard Senter, Robert J. Thaler, Carolyn Vanderslice, Sam Vuchinich, Brinson Williams, Lyn Woods, and Eugene Won.

Each of these students carried out one or more of the

following tasks: preparation of a research memorandum suggesting and evaluating items for inclusion in the survey; conducting pretest interviews; screening and evaluating questions on the basis of pretest results; conducting 12–15 interviews; and writing an analytical paper on a particular topic in the 1971 study. We want to emphasize the intellectual as well as logistical contribution made by the students. As a consequence of their work, the amount of forethought and critical evaluation incorporated into our study design was quite unusual.

The exacting work of designing most of the code structure and supervising the coding was ably handled by Elizabeth Fischer with the assistance of Sunny Bradford. Fischer also carried primary responsibility for organizing the retrieval of data from the base-line studies. Assistance in computer programing and computation was provided by J. Michael Coble, Juliet Umberger, R. W. Nylund, Mark Evers, Eugene Won, Shirley J. Hatchett, James Carr, and Viola Stafford.

A substantial part of the 1971 survey—sample design, part of the interviewing, and coding—was carried out by professional staff of the Survey Research Center, University of Michigan. Without their technical advice and assistance, a field survey of this scope could not have been carried out.

Finally, we should like to acknowledge the general support provided by the Population Studies Center of the University of Michigan for our research activities. This, too, was a sine qua non of the project.